剑桥双语分级阅读·小说馆（第2版）

原版系列编辑 **Philip Prowse**

A Matter of Chance 意外人生

[英] 戴维·希尔 著

王文赞 编译

郭建民 审订

北京语言大学出版社
BEIJING LANGUAGE AND CULTURE UNIVERSITY PRESS

CAMBRIDGE UNIVERSITY PRESS

社图号25005

北京市版权局著作权合同登记图字：01-2024-3256号

图书在版编目（CIP）数据

意外人生 ： 英汉对照 / （英） 戴维·希尔 (David Hill) 著 ； 王文赞编译. -- 2版. -- 北京 ： 北京语言大学出版社, 2025. 3. -- （剑桥双语分级阅读小说馆）. -- ISBN 978-7-5619-6724-9

Ⅰ. H319.4

中国国家版本馆CIP数据核字第2025F0R276号

意外人生
YIWAI RENSHENG

责任编辑：李　珍
责任印制：周　燚

出版发行：北京语言大学出版社
社　　址：北京市海淀区学院路 15 号，100083
网　　址：www.blcup.com
电子信箱：service@blcup.com
电　　话：编 辑 部 010-8230 1019
发 行 部 010-8230 3650/3591/3648
北语书店 010-8230 3653
网购咨询 010-8230 3908
印　　刷：东港股份有限公司

版　　次：2017 年 6 月第 1 版　2025 年 3 月第 2 版
印　　次：2025 年 3 月第 1 次印刷
开　　本：880 毫米 × 1230 毫米　1/32
印　　张：5.625
字　　数：134 千字
定　　价：23.00 元

PRINTED IN CHINA
凡有印装质量问题，本社负责调换。售后QQ号1367565611，电话010-82303590

Preface

前言

“剑桥双语分级阅读·小说馆”是一套从剑桥大学出版社引进的面向非英语国家英语学习者的分级系列读物，由英语语言教学专家及小说作家合力创作。创作过程历时三十余年，出版后受到世界各地英语教师和英语学习者的喜爱，许多读本再版多次，三十余年来畅销不衰，成为受全球英语学习者青睐的优秀读本。

本系列读物具有以下突出特色：

1. 是原创英语读物，而非改编自普通作品的读物。因此，阅读本系列读物，我们读到的是原汁原味的原创英语，而非人为改编过的二手英语。

2. 是当代优秀短篇小说，而非年代久远的小说。因此，阅读本系列读物，我们读到的是当今鲜活的、学了就能用的英语，而非穿越时空的、学了用不上的英语；了解的是与读者同时代不同国家人们的生活和思想，而非隔代人的生活、文化和风土人情。

3. 是专为非英语国家的英语学习者量身定制的读物，而非为英语母语者所写的大众读物。因此，本系列读物是中国读者首选的英语学习读物。

4. 是英美知名小说家和英语语言教学专家合力创作的读物。小说家保障了读物的可读性与可欣赏性，英语语言教学专家保障了读物语言作为英语习得材料的科学性与可学性。本系列读物中的多个读本都曾在世界上颇具影响力的“语言学习者文学奖”（Language Learner Literature Award）评选中获得大奖。因此，阅读本系列读物，我们会在欣赏小说的同时，自然而然地、有效地提高自己的英语水平。

5. 本系列读物的故事题材丰富多样，包括侦探、情感、历险、悬疑、人文、科幻、喜剧等，读者可以随心选择自己喜欢的类别阅读；故事内容生动有趣，故事情节引人入胜、扣人心弦，读者一旦开始阅读，就想一口气读完，使阅读真正升华到“悦读”。

6. 随书附赠的音频材料内容精彩，是专业配音员的演绎再创作。听着它，我们犹如在听广播剧、听评书，又仿佛是在听电影、听话剧……这种聆听英语的享受将彻底扫除学生对英语听力的畏难心理。

7. 本系列读物所使用的语言，既有英式英语，也有美式英语，对应的音频材料也相应分为英音和美音，读者可根据自己的喜好来选择。

8. 本系列近百本读物根据《欧洲语言共同参考框架》(CEFR)和剑桥大学外语考评部开发的 ESOL 考试的标准来确定级别划分，是建立在科学研究和实践基础之上的分级。全套共分七个级别（与中国学生英语基础水平的大致对应关系，请参见图书封底表格），读者可根据自己的英语基础选择相应级别的读本来学习。

为了更好地帮助中国学生学习和欣赏，“剑桥双语分级阅读·小说馆”从剑桥大学出版社原版引进后又增加了以下内容：

1. 增加了适量的辅助学习内容，包括“读前思考”“读后活动”“学习指导”三个板块，其中“学习指导”板块又包括生词、短语和表达、文化点滴、阅读练习四项内容。增加这些板块的目的是全方位帮助学生提升英语阅读能力，扩充词汇量，扫除阅读中的文化障碍，增强对英语小说的鉴赏能力。

2. 增加了小说全文的参考译文。出于语言学习的考虑，译文多采用直译，但也尽量符合中文的表达习惯。

值得一提的是，所增加的辅助学习内容和参考译文，全部由来自全国不同省市知名中学（包括人大附中、北大附中、清华附中、黄冈中学、上海中学等三十余所中学）的一线英语教师完成。这些一线教师的加盟，确保了所加内容与中国学生的英语学习特点和学习需求相吻合，为学生阅读和欣赏读物、提高英语水平给予恰到好处的助力。

英语阅读是英语课堂的延伸和补充，也是培养英语语感、提高英语水平的有效途径。选择一套好的英语读物，收获的将不仅仅是语言的进步。欢迎年轻朋友们来到“剑桥双语分级阅读·小说馆”，打开一本本好书，品味一个个好故事，为实现梦想搭建桥梁。

北京语言大学出版社

Contents 目录

People in the story

故事中的人物

Paul Morris: a marketing manager for pharmaceutical companies, first in Manchester, England, then in Italy.

保罗·莫里斯：制药公司的一名销售经理，先在英国的曼彻斯特工作，后在意大利工作。

Jacky Morris: Paul's wife, a marketing manager for the same pharmaceutical companies.

杰基·莫里斯：保罗的妻子，同一家制药公司的销售经理。

Sandra Rovello: works for an Italian pharmaceutical company.

桑德拉·罗韦洛：在一家意大利制药公司工作。

Mr and Mrs Rovello: Sandra's parents. Mr Rovello manages an import-export furniture company.
罗韦洛夫妇：桑德拉的父母。罗韦洛先生经营了一家进出口家具公司。

Andrea Carta: a business partner of Mr Rovello's.
安德里亚·卡尔塔：罗韦洛先生的一个商业伙伴。

Before reading

读前思考

1. Look at the front cover and the back cover blurb. What sort of story do you think this will be?

2. Read the Contents on page 1. Imagine what might happen in the story.

3. Look at the list of characters on pages 2 and 3. What do you think they look like?

4. If you have the recording, listen to Chapter 1.

Chapter 1
The roof-tile

The roof-tile fell.

* * *

After two or three hundred years of rain, ice, snow, wind and sun the roof-tile fell.

* * *

After two or three hundred years of rain, ice, snow, wind and sun the roof-tile fell from its place down into the street of the old town.

* * *

After two or three hundred years of rain, ice, snow, wind and sun the roof-tile fell from its place down into the street of the old town and hit my wife in the middle of her head.

* * *

After two or three hundred years of rain, ice, snow, wind and sun the roof-tile fell from its place down into the street of the old town and hit my wife in the middle of her head, killing her instantly.

Chapter 2
Jacky

Jacky.

What can I tell you about Jacky?

I can tell you how she looked that bright February morning when she stepped out into the new sun, as the snow was falling off all the roofs, as she went out to buy something for a dress she was making. For a special dinner – we had been married for three years.

I have a film library of her in the back of my head: in the office; our first Christmas together, skiing in Scotland; the wedding; the trip across France to our new home in Italy; and ... and ... I also have ten photographs of her that I took. Just ten out of the hundreds.

Afterwards, when I was able to, I looked through all the photos of our life together and carefully chose the ten I liked the best. I then had them enlarged, and put them in a special photo album. Which I have never opened since. All this was many years ago. I am an old man now.

An old man full of memories, and full of thoughts

about what could have been. An old man who often thinks about the way that one tiny chance happening can change someone's life: the roof-tile falls a second earlier or a second later, she goes towards a different shop, she goes towards the same shop a different way, she meets a friend and stops to talk, she doesn't meet a friend and stop to talk, the traffic lights change as she gets to the crossing ... or ... or ...

Such a little tiny chance that she was there then and the roof-tile was there then. Such a little tiny chance that left me, at twenty-seven years of age, alone in a foreign country. Italy. So much hope. Such a bright future. Such an exciting thing to do. An adventure. To go and start a new life in Italy.

Jacky and I had met at work in Manchester. We had started at the same time. We enjoyed being together at first because we were both new there, and it was good to have someone in the same situation to talk to. Talk at work led to talk in pubs, days out at weekends, and by November we were in love and planning a first skiing holiday in Scotland ... the first time together, the first time away with someone I really loved.

After that things moved quickly. We got engaged to be married on her twenty-fourth birthday (January 20) and got married at Easter. We then spent two more years working in Manchester, during which time we decided that we wanted a change. We'd visited Italy twice in those years. Once we'd toured around the northern lakes in a car, and once we'd stayed in a farmhouse in Umbria.

We fell in love with Italy the first moment we got there, for all the usual romantic reasons – the sun, the scenery, the food and wine, the people, the buildings. It seemed right for us. We went to Italian evening classes in Manchester, and got quite good at the language.

'*Io mi chiamo Paul Morris, e tu sei la mia moglie, Jacky*' I used to sing around the house. We watched Italian films at the Arts Centre, and we went to Italian restaurants regularly.

We wanted a change. Three years in Manchester was enough. Jacky came from Norwich and I came from Bedford, so neither of us had any reason to stay in Manchester except the job and each other. And then that special day came. One Friday evening I was reading the 'Abroad' part of the APPOINTMENTS section in the weekly company newspaper, when one advertisement jumped off the page at me:

> **CORVO PHARMACEUTICALS**
> Well-established company in Como needs two enthusiastic young marketing managers to start September 1st.
> Accommodation provided.
> Return airfare paid.
>
> Tel: Mrs Robinson on
> 0183-7674321 for further details.

I remember running into the kitchen with the paper shouting 'Jacky! Jacky! Como!' and nearly knocking her down in my excitement.

We'd been to Como two years earlier and we'd loved both the town and the lake. And now here was a job in that wonderful place!

Jacky was soon more excited than me, and phoned Mrs Robinson at once. We couldn't sleep that night, talking about all the wonderful possibilities if we could get the job. The following Monday the application forms and details about the job arrived. It all sounded perfect. The company was a good one, and they provided a flat in the centre of the old town. To cut a long story short, we applied for the jobs, we were given interviews and in late May, we were offered the jobs. And we accepted.

Italy. We were going to live there. Out of cold wet Manchester and into those hot summers, the blue lake, the snowy winters, the beautiful scenery, the skiing ... it was all going to be ours all the time!

We left our jobs. Everyone, our friends and family, even the people at work, thought we were silly to leave good jobs in England for an uncertain life abroad. We had expected that. We didn't mind. We packed our things, left some things with our parents and sent other things to Italy by train. In mid-August we took a two-week holiday and drove through France by car on our way to Como.

We arrived at the end of August to get the flat ready before starting work in September. It was three years after we'd met in Manchester. What a lot of changes in such a short time!

Even now, after all these years, I can still remember exactly how good it felt to be in Como. Jacky and Italy, I used to say to myself, the two loves of my life, and I had them both! What a lucky man!

And I knew that Jacky felt just the same. Our love for each other grew stronger. We did everything together. Work and play. We were closer than ever before. We really enjoyed our work. The Italians we worked with were wonderful and we made friends easily. And at home all the neighbours were welcoming and helpful. It all seemed perfect.

And then, five months later, she wasn't there any more. I would never see her grey eyes shining up at me again; her hair on the pillow, like in that song by Leonard Cohen – 'a sleepy golden storm'. Nothing. Just me.

Chapter 3
Sandra

What do you do when a big hole suddenly appears in your life? You either fall into it, or you start to fill it up.

Jacky was buried back home in England. To me, it all seemed to happen in a bad dream. Everything that happened after that seemed like a dream too.

There were a lot of papers to fill in, meetings to go to and trips back to England. But there was one thing clear in my head: I wanted to stay in Como. Jacky would have wanted me to stay. That was a good dream I didn't want to let go of. My family and Jacky's family thought I should return to Britain, to be with the people I knew well, people who cared about me. I knew that was not right. That felt like I was running away. I had to return and do things my own way.

So, two weeks after Jacky was buried, I went straight back to Como and back to work. I worked hard. I often worked all day and then stayed at the office late. Sometimes I took my work home in the evening. I even took over some of Jacky's work to help the company and to fill up more of my empty time.

At weekends I drove somewhere in the mountains and skied all day until I was exhausted. People were kind. I got lots of invitations from the people I worked with, but I didn't accept many of them. I went on short holidays alone, holidays that I had already planned with Jacky ...

I suppose the friendship with Sandra started in February. Sandra had worked in Jacky's team. She didn't look a lot like Jacky, but ... perhaps I was just lonely. I knew her well enough to say '*Ciao*' in the office and I'd gone out with the team for a pizza before the Christmas holidays. Once or twice I'd found myself looking at her. Once she'd seen me and given me a smile in return.

But I wanted to be alone with my memories of Jacky. One night in January I was walking home from work and met Sandra. We talked as we walked along the winter streets. And when we said goodbye ten minutes later – a warm handshake in the cold evening – I realised that my heart was beating faster than usual and my face was hot. I felt like a boy out on his first date!

Then I forgot all about Sandra again. In February I

took over Jacky's marketing team. At our first meeting, when I walked into the room, there was Sandra, sitting right in front of me. I almost couldn't speak at first.

Sandra was very helpful during the meeting – the kind of person all managers need when they're new to a group. And at the end of the meeting she stayed behind when the others had gone. She came up to me.

'Paul,' she said, 'I wanted to tell you how very sorry I am about Jacky.' And then she did a surprising thing. She kissed me lightly on my cheek and was gone, leaving me with the smell of her perfume and the feel of her soft lips on my skin. I felt very confused.

That night at home I cried for the first time since Jacky's death. I cried for hours, thinking about my whole life with her, all the good moments, and the emptiness I knew I'd really been trying to cover up. I have never cried as much before or since. For her. For us. For our dream. For me ... Then I realised that I couldn't continue living and working and going on holiday as though Jacky was still alive. When I went into the bathroom the next morning, and looked at my red eyes and my white face, I thought that it was the start of my new life after Jacky's death.

And it was Sandra who had helped me with that.

Yes, in the end, I could say Sandra helped me. Despite everything that happened with me and Sandra, she helped me at that time. That kiss after the meeting had changed something inside me. And change was what I needed after losing Jacky.

I spoke to Sandra after the next meeting, and we walked part of the way through the town together, talking. It became something I looked forward to. I prepared for those group meetings especially well and my new team worked hard. And I knew that at the end of each afternoon meeting I would have a few minutes' walk with Sandra.

At Easter I went on a tour of the villas of Veneto, a tour I had planned with Jacky and I went alone. I often thought of Jacky, of how she would have enjoyed it, but I also thought of Sandra. I sent Sandra a postcard from Veneto. I'd only found out her address because I wanted to see where she lived in Como. But in the darkness of those cheap hotels on my own, after a day of looking at brilliant architecture, I often found myself thinking of her. I pictured her in the office – the smile on her full lips, the dark brown eyes and shoulder-length dark brown hair. In my mind I replayed her light kiss again and again like a film. And I realised I was beginning to wonder what it would be like to kiss her properly, to hold her ...

I have to say that I felt guilty about those thoughts. After all it was only four months since Jacky had died.

But I couldn't stop thinking about Sandra. So I sent her a postcard, and signed it, *Love, Paul.*

Chapter 4
A weekend in the country

And then in late April, after another of our team meetings, on our now usual walk through town together, she suddenly asked, 'Paul, what are you doing next weekend?'

'Nothing special,' I replied. 'Why?'

'Would you like to come to my family's old house in Magreglio, up in the mountains? It would be good for you to get out of Como.'

I replied at once. 'I'd love to.' I was quite surprised to hear myself answer so quickly. But I was even more surprised when she put her hands on the sides of my face and kissed me on my mouth. I didn't really kiss back, at first, but then I put my arms around her waist and it turned into a long, deep kiss. And it felt so good. Like something I'd always been waiting for. So warm and full. So exciting. Like eating a strange new fruit.

I then walked her all the way home for the first time, stopping for several more kisses on the way, and making plans for the weekend.

Back in my flat I felt as if I was walking on air. Feelings of guilt and excitement mixed – as if I was having a relationship and my wife didn't know. I couldn't sleep. It was a beautiful night, so I took a bottle of white wine out of the fridge and sat on the balcony. I drank the wine and watched the moon rise over the mountains ... A new life was opening up.

It was pouring with rain when Sandra arrived in her car at nine o'clock on Saturday morning, as arranged. I was ready and ran out of the flat entrance into her car, and into a long kiss. I was so excited that I hardly noticed that the car was a very expensive Alfa Romeo – far bigger than she could have afforded on her salary at Corvo Pharmaceuticals.

There was some kind of electricity between us in the car as we drove along the lakeside road, with heavy rain hiding both the lake and mountains. It made the world inside the car even stranger and more cut off from everything else. I asked her about the house we were going to – she'd not said much when we'd made the arrangements, just that it would be cold at night and to bring warm clothes and walking boots. It had, she said, belonged to her great-grandparents first. Her parents had lived there when they were first married, but now it was just a place to escape to at weekends.

She and her brother had stopped going there much in the last few years. They'd wanted to travel and see other places. Como and Magreglio were not all there was. She laughed. I loved her laugh, so natural and free. An hour later we were there, parking the car under the trees and walking up the wet path past the vegetable garden, in the rain, up to the house. It was very dark inside.

'Where are your parents?' I asked.

'In Como,' she replied. 'Why?'

'Well, I thought they'd be here, doing weekend gardening and things,' I answered, still rather surprised. The old family house, she'd said, and I'd thought the family would be there.

She turned round, very slowly, and walked over to stand in front of me, her eyes almost black in the low light, but shining, and said, 'Why would I have wanted to bring you if they were here?'

I said something stupid like, 'Oh, I see,' and tried to put my arms around her. She pushed me off, playfully.

'Later,' she said. 'Let's make this place warm first.'

And for the next hour she was busy turning on the heaters in all the rooms while I made a wood fire in the living room. Then we put the food we'd brought in the fridge, and she made coffee. We sat on the sofa drinking it as the fire grew bigger. It was half past eleven.

'Let me show you round now,' she said, and took me on a tour of the house. There was a big living room, a kitchen-dining room, and a modern bathroom downstairs, and three small bedrooms under the roof upstairs.

'This was my bedroom when I was a little girl,' she said in the smallest upstairs room. 'I used to lie here and watch the sun come up over that mountain every morning in summer ... and look, the sun's coming out now! Let me show you the garden.'

We put our boots on because it was still very wet on the ground outside. We walked hand-in-hand as she showed me where her grandparents had kept chickens, what vegetables her parents were growing this year, the apple tree where she'd played as a girl.

'What's down there?' I asked, pointing to some stone steps going down to a brown door in the side of the house.

'Oh, nothing now,' she said. 'It was where they used to put wine and vegetables sometimes.'

I was just turning away when I noticed the lock on the door – it was new.

'But Sandra ...' I started. She was already walking back to the house saying something about lunch. She put together one of those delicious simple meals Italians can always make in no time, and we ate it with the good red wine I had brought ... for her parents! She disappeared while I put more wood on the dying fire. I looked out of the window. The rain was pouring down again. I had hoped we would go for a walk to the village after lunch, but I didn't feel like it in that rain.

'It's raining again, Sandra,' I called. 'What shall we do this afternoon?'

There was no answer. I went into the kitchen – she wasn't there. I thought she'd probably gone to the bathroom, so I went back into the warm living room.

'Paul,' I heard. 'Paul, can you just come up here a moment?' I climbed the stairs wondering what the problem was. The largest bedroom door was open, so I went inside. 'What did you want ... ?' Sandra was lying on the bed, smiling.

'I thought this might be a good place to spend a wet Saturday afternoon,' she said.

'Well, it looks more fun than the village in the rain,' I managed to say.

Looking back now, it was perhaps the most

enjoyable weekend I've ever had. And I've had a few relationships since then. We never did see Magreglio that weekend, nor much of the rest of the house, except for trips to get food or wine from the kitchen!

When I got back to the flat in Como on the Sunday night, I felt deeply physically tired and very happy in a completely new way. Not that I wanted to compare Jacky, but being with Sandra was like a new, adult adventure rather than the more innocent love I'd known before with Jacky.

Chapter 5
Mystery in Switzerland

'Let's go to Lugano this afternoon,' said Sandra suddenly. We were just finishing lunch one late June Saturday. Since our trip to Magreglio we'd spent several weekends and many evenings and nights together, mostly in my flat. She still lived with her parents in Como.

'What?' I asked in surprise. Usually, in the afternoons, we would drive to Belaggio to eat cakes, or to Villa Carlotta for a walk in the gardens. 'Why should we go to Switzerland?'

'For a change,' she replied. 'Have you ever been? It's not far, you know.'

'I know. Jacky and I went last November.' By then I could talk about Jacky as if our marriage had finished years ago, not just months ago. Sandra had changed everything.

'And you can drive us in your car, too,' she said.

'OK,' I agreed, happy for the opportunity of

driving – she usually drove us everywhere, saying that she knew the roads better. And her Alfa Romeo was much nicer.

'Let's take your car,' I said.

'It's not working at the moment,' she said. I didn't think then she had a reason to use my car to drive to Switzerland. It was only later that I understood.

'But take me home first,' she went on. 'I need to get something.'

After driving up to Belaggio, we took the ferry over Lake Como to Menaggio then up over the hill and down to Lake Lugano. Next we went along the lakeside road to the customs. There the Italian officers let us straight through the border, but the Swiss officers checked our passports and asked us where we were going. We then continued round to Lugano and parked the car.

We kissed and then walked along to one of the extremely tidy cafés in the square. We ordered two of the large bowls of fruit, ice-cream and cream which the Swiss like so much.

After a few moments, Sandra looked around the square, looked at her watch and then stood up. 'Toilet,' she said and disappeared inside the café. The ice-creams arrived and I started eating mine, wondering why Sandra was taking so long. After five minutes I stood up to see where she was. I couldn't see her inside the café. So for some reason I looked over the pots of flowers and into the part of the square behind where we were sitting ... and there was Sandra, about a hundred metres away.

She was talking seriously to a very well-dressed man with a bald head and designer sunglasses, who was standing next to a silver Mercedes. The man was obviously quite angry. I saw Sandra open her bag and give him a small package. She then said something else, then turned to walk back to our café.

I sat down again and ate some ice-cream. My heart was beating fast and I wondered what was going on. The surprise trip to Lugano, using my car, meeting the rich man, the package ... it was like something out of a spy film! I didn't know if I should ask Sandra about it or not.

'Sorry, Paul,' she said when she got back to the table, giving me a kiss on the cheek. 'There was a queue, and then I took too long doing my make-up.'

'Eat your ice-cream. It's melting,' I heard myself say. Apparently I had decided to be cool and try to find out what was happening later on.

Chapter 6
The summer holidays

During the summer in Italy, everything seems to slow down. Most people go on holiday to the beach or the mountains. I hadn't really thought about what to do in the holidays. Jacky and I had talked about driving around southern Italy by car, and although I still liked the idea, I didn't want to do it alone.

It was Sandra who mentioned the subject of holidays, about one week after the Lugano trip. We were in bed in my flat in Como when she turned to me with a serious face and said, 'What are you doing this summer, Paul?'

'I haven't really thought about it,' I answered truthfully. 'What are you doing?'

'Well, I usually spend the first two weeks at our family place at the seaside. It's in Portofino. Have you ever been there?'

'No,' I replied, 'But I've seen some pictures. It's very beautiful.'

'Would you like to come down?' she asked.

'Well ... er ... yes. That would be lovely. But ... er ... where would I stay?'

'Oh, there's plenty of space,' she answered. 'We'll find you a bed.'

'We?' I asked.

'Oh, yes. All the family will be there, this time,' she said, and added, 'Not like at Magreglio!'

'Oh, I see,' I replied, feeling a little disappointed. But I said yes. Of course I said yes. Why would I say no? She was beautiful and I was in a beautiful country. If I had known what was going to happen I would have said no. Definitely.

Sandra left for Portofino a few days before me. I decided I would visit a few places on my drive down from Como to Portofino. I visited Florence, Lucca and Pisa in Tuscany, before driving north along the coast until I got to Portofino. The narrow roads were heavy with summer traffic, but the scenery was beautiful – green hills covered in trees going straight down into the blue waters of the Mediterranean Sea.

The place itself had once been a fishing village, and there was a group of red and yellow buildings along the sea, with a castle on the other side. The water was full of boats, many of which were luxury yachts. It was wonderful in the strong summer afternoon light.

I couldn't wait to see Sandra. I hadn't seen her in over a week and I was rather surprised to find just how much I was missing her. I realised how important she had become to me since Jacky's death.

And also I still didn't understand her. That locked room at Magreglio, the expensive car she drove, the trip to Lugano and the mysterious meeting and the package; the fact that she'd never told me about her life outside work. (She'd once said that there was a 'family business' which was 'import-export' and that she sometimes helped.)

There was something else that I really only thought about as I was driving down through Italy: why couldn't she see me on two or three occasions? She had said something about 'having to go away somewhere' without explaining anything. I didn't ask too many questions though. It never seemed the right place or the right time. I also felt that if I asked too many questions – about the Lugano package, for example – that she would stop our relationship, and I'd be alone again. And I wasn't sure I wanted to be alone again just now. I also hoped I might find some answers to these questions when I got to Portofino ...

I eventually found the right road. It was almost at the top of the hill. Number 19, Via Cadorna – the Villa Bellavista. It had a wonderful view over the sea to the castle. I imagined that her family had a flat in the large building, presumably once the holiday home of some rich businessman. Sandra's shining Alfa Romeo, a couple of Mercedes and a bright yellow Fiat sports car were in a parking area next to a large garden. Quite a place!

I parked my dirty old British Metro next to Sandra's car and got out. At the door I couldn't find any surnames to show me which flat was which, so I rang the only bell I could find. The door was answered by a middle-aged woman dressed as a housekeeper.

'Yes?' she asked coldly, looking me up and down.

'Does Sandra Rovello live here?' I asked.

'Miss Alessandra is out. Who shall I say called?' she replied.

'Well, my name's Paul. Paul Morris, and Sandra is ...' I didn't have to find the right words because there was the noise of a car turning into the drive which made us both turn. My mouth fell open when I realised that it was Sandra, sitting in the silver

Mercedes with the man I'd seen her meet in Lugano.

Sandra looked at my dirty car, then across to where I was standing with the housekeeper, and her face was very serious. I walked over to her as she got out of the car.

'Oh, Paul,' she said, smiling weakly. 'How nice. Look, Andrea – here's Paul Morris, my new manager at Corvo. Paul, please meet Andrea Carta.'

It was a difficult situation. I tried to be polite, but I was quite embarrassed as I shook his hand. Andrea just looked at me in an uninterested way.

'I'm going inside, Alessandra,' he said. 'I'll see you later. Goodbye, Mr Morris. Nice to have met you.'

I stood in the lovely garden, in front of the fine villa, with a beautiful young Italian woman, and I had no idea what to think, what to say or what to do. I stared at the ground.

'Paul,' Sandra said when Andrea had gone in, 'let's walk in the garden.' I couldn't say anything. She came and took my hand.

'Come and tell me all about your holidays,' she said. 'What did you visit?'

I didn't really want to, but I walked into the back garden with her and we sat on a seat near a pool full of fish. I felt like one of them, going round and round in circles without understanding where I was.

'Paul,' she said, trying to take my hand, 'why are you so upset?'

'Well, how else should I feel? You invited me here, and then you ... you ... you come driving in with another man,' I replied.

'But there's nothing between us, Paul,' she said. 'He's just a friend of the family. Nothing more.' I turned and looked into her eyes.

'Sandra, I saw you meet him in Lugano,' I said simply.

'Oh ... he's ... er ...' she started.

'Just forget it, Sandra,' I said quietly, and tried to stand up. She pulled me back onto the bench.

'My father just wanted me to give him something,' she said. 'They do business sometimes, Paul. Honestly! Nothing more,' she said.

'Really?' I asked suspiciously.

'Really,' she answered. And then she kissed me. I realise now that she probably kissed me to shut me up, so she wouldn't have to explain anything else. But then I suppose I was feeling so strange about everything — my life — that I kissed her back, long and hard.

'I'm sorry, Paul,' she said again.

'Well, I'd better go. Your father's friend obviously didn't want me around.'

'No, you can't. You must stay now you've come. Don't worry about him. He's just like that. Come on,' she said, taking my hand. 'Let's go and get your things and find you a room.'

Chapter 7
Getting in deeper

At eight thirty that evening I came down from my room for pre-dinner drinks with Sandra's parents. Andrea and two other men were introduced as old business partners of her father. There were also two big men, who looked like bodyguards, but they were introduced as workers in the family business. Everyone was very polite and I thanked them for inviting me to stay.

'Oh, don't mention it,' said Mrs Rovello, who was covered in gold jewellery. 'We're so pleased that you could come and visit us. Sandra has been saying wonderful things about you. She has often told us how helpful you have been with her business studies.'

I smiled and thanked her and then looked across at Sandra. Business studies! What had she been telling them? She looked so innocent and calm. She smiled to me and then refilled my glass. Dinner was long and the food was excellent, with local fish as the main course. After dinner Mr Rovello said he had things to talk over, and took the other men into another room, saying, 'Help yourself to drinks, watch TV,' as he closed the door.

Sandra's mother disappeared, and Sandra and I were left alone. I poured myself a very large whisky from one of the bottles on the sideboard, and, taking a mouthful, said, 'So, what's going on? Shall we talk about all this?'

Sandra came up to me and gave me a small kiss on my cheek. I sat down. I understood nothing. I looked around the room. Expensive antique furniture, a painting by Giorgio Morandi on the wall, Murano glass ... The Rovellos were seriously rich.

'In the morning,' she said. She took my hand and led me upstairs to my bedroom. At the door she said, 'Different rooms, I'm afraid. I'm tired now. Goodnight.' Then she kissed me quickly and she was gone.

In my room I sat down and drank my whisky. There was a TV in the room and I turned it on and looked through the channels – there were the usual Saturday night programmes – game-shows and old films, none of which I was interested in. I kept thinking of Sandra in another room, getting undressed, getting into bed, and of how much I wanted her.

I knew I couldn't sleep immediately, so I decided to get a breath of fresh air. I went downstairs very quietly and out a side door, leaving it open so that I could get back in.

The garden was still warm from the sun and smelt lovely. It was a beautiful night. I walked round the house and suddenly found myself below a room with open windows. I could hear voices coming from inside.

'... And that's why she invited him here ...' Andrea was saying.

'Yes, but it's very dangerous in this situation,' Mr Rovello was saying.

'Oh, no. I don't think so,' said Andrea. 'He obviously doesn't know about anything. Look how easy the Lugano job was. It was a very clever idea.'

'Well, we were still lucky,' argued Mr Rovello.

'But do you think Sandra will be able to persuade him to go to England?' asked one of the business partners.

'I think he'll do anything she asks him,' replied Andrea.

I couldn't believe what I was hearing. I listened hard to catch every word.

'Good, because if we can get our things through to London quickly, now that Andrea's American connection has been closed down, it might help us to keep our hands on that market ...' said one of the partners.

'But he must know nothing,' said Andrea. 'Alessandra needs to ...'

That was the last thing I heard of their conversation, but I didn't know that until I woke up in my room an hour or so later. I was lying in bed. Sandra was sitting beside me. I had a wet towel on my head and a terrible headache.

'You're going to have to rest for a while,' she said. 'Stupid boy!'

I couldn't see very clearly. 'What happened?' I asked.

'Oh, poor Paul. What were you doing outside the house in the dark? One of the bodyguards thought you were a burglar. He didn't realise you were a guest of the family.'

'Well, there was no need for him to hit me,' I said, gently touching my head.

'I know. I'm sorry. The guards are not very gentle, I'm afraid. But now, Paul, you've got to get some sleep,' said Sandra, putting down the towel and drying her hands.

'But Sandra ... ' I started.

'Not now, Paul,' she replied. 'Go to sleep and we'll talk about it in the morning.'

And she kissed me on the top of my head and went, leaving me in the dark room with a headache, and more questions than when I'd arrived at Villa Bellavista a few hours earlier.

As I lay there, I turned everything around in my head. I was very frightened. I felt like an animal that has been caught. What did these people want from me? Should I get up and leave now? How could I get out of this horrible situation? Damn Sandra! Damn Jacky! Damn that roof-tile! My angry thoughts brought me back to reality. I couldn't blame my dead wife. This was my fault. I had been so interested in Sandra, I had needed her so much after Jacky's death that I hadn't thought clearly about anything. Eventually, I fell asleep.

Chapter 8
Preparations

I woke early. It was about four o'clock. I needed some air, so I went onto the balcony outside my room. It was still dark, but I could hear the sea. I looked across to the castle which had lights shining on it. The wind was playing with the trees. It was very beautiful. As I stood there, I heard a noise below me. I looked down. I was just in time to see one of the bodyguards standing close to my car. Unfortunately it was still quite dark in the car park, so I couldn't see exactly what he was doing. But it didn't make me very happy.

From what I'd heard about 'the American connection' and 'getting things through to London', I thought I had finally found out what the 'family business' was: selling drugs or something else illegal. And when I put what I'd heard this evening together with what I'd seen before – the locked room at Magreglio, the package in Lugano – it appeared quite clear now. Why hadn't I thought about it before? Why hadn't I said anything in Lugano? I thought how stupid I'd been to let myself get into this mess. And now I also understood something else.

It seemed that Sandra had been using me all along. She had already used me once to take something – drugs, perhaps, or gold – to Lugano. And in my car. Just imagine if we'd been caught! And she had only invited me here because she wanted to persuade me to go with her to England with something else – something that was even more important. How stupid I had been!

I went back into my room, and after lying, thinking about all of the strange things I had seen and heard, I finally went to sleep again. At about ten o'clock I was woken by Sandra with some coffee and rolls.

'Hello,' she said brightly, as she opened the curtains. 'How do you feel this morning?'

'OK, I suppose,' I replied, feeling my head carefully.

'Well, here's some nice breakfast for you,' she said, smiling. 'When you're ready come and find me in the garden by the pool. I've got something I want to talk about.'

'Sandra ...' I started, but she had already gone. So I had my breakfast, got myself ready and went down into the heat of the Mediterranean garden to find Sandra. When she saw me coming, she got up and came towards me.

'Hello, Paul,' she said, taking my hand. 'You look much better. I'm so sorry about last night.'

'Are you?' I replied suspiciously. We sat on the seat by the pool again, and she kissed my cheek. I felt very uncertain about what to do and say after everything that had happened.

'Of course I am,' she said. 'How are you feeling now?'

'OK,' I said. She kissed me again.

'Good. Because I've just had a great idea. We've got a lot of time before we have to go back to work in Como. Why don't we go to England?'

'Why should we?' I asked simply. I wondered what she would answer after what I had heard last night. And I also wondered exactly what she knew about the 'family business'.

'You could show me everything. We could have a little holiday together in England. What do you say?'

I thought for a long time before I spoke.

'I would like to go to England with you Sandra. Very much. I enjoy being with you, and you're really the only friend I've got. But I need the answers to one or two questions before we go.'

'What questions, Paul?' she asked.

'I need to know about Andrea, about what happened in Lugano, about what I heard last night,' I said. 'And I need some honest answers.'

'I've told you about Andrea,' Sandra said. 'He's simply one of my father's business partners. He manages our exports to the USA, but there have been some problems there recently. That's why he's here talking to my father this weekend.'

'So why did we go to Lugano that time?' I asked.

'For an afternoon out,' she said, 'and because my father asked me to meet Andrea and give him something he'd forgotten.'

'What was it?' I asked, staring at her hard. She stared back.

'I don't know, Paul,' she answered. 'Papers, or something. I work for Corvo Pharmaceuticals, not my father's business. It was nothing to do with me. I was just doing something for my father.'

She seemed to be telling the truth. Maybe I was just imagining everything. Perhaps I had watched too many James Bond films when I was younger!

Or perhaps I just wanted to believe her. I looked at her. She was very beautiful. I found it very difficult to see her as a criminal. Perhaps they had just been talking about normal business last night, but then why did the guard hit me?

'Yes, but why did that guard hit me last night?' I asked.

'I told you,' Sandra replied. 'He thought you were a burglar. They get very nervous. It looked suspicious. Anyway, how is your poor head now?'

She reached up and turned my head to look at the place where I'd been hit. Then she turned my face towards her and kissed me.

'It looks much better now,' she said. 'So, shall we go to England or not?'

I took a deep breath.

'All right,' I said.

'Good. Let's go tomorrow,' she said. 'I want to get away from here as soon as possible!'

Chapter 9
Into France

By ten o'clock the next morning we were already driving along the motorway west of Genoa, nearing the French border. Light shone off the sea and onto the surrounding hills. The journey had been easy so far. When we got to the border itself, however, we met unexpected queues of slowly moving traffic. As we came up to the customs buildings there were policemen everywhere wearing special clothes and carrying sub-machine guns.

My heart jumped. Perhaps I was involved in something illegal after all! Perhaps I was going to be caught and finish in prison! I looked at Sandra. She was chewing her lip and looking nervous.

But the police just waved us through. Obviously they were looking for someone else. Sandra looked much less worried when the cars began to increase speed on the French side of the border. I was starting to feel suspicious again. Her behaviour had not been normal for someone who was just on holiday with her boyfriend. Perhaps we were carrying something in the car after all.

'Sandra,' I said, 'are you sure we're not doing something illegal?'

'Why?' she asked. 'What do you mean?'

'Well, it's just that you looked so nervous at the border back there with the police ...'

'Oh, please, Paul!' she said. 'I'm tired of all your questions. Don't be so suspicious.' She wasn't so sweet to me now.

After that we didn't speak for a long time. The motorway was quite busy as we drove near the famous tourist resorts of Cannes and Nice, and through the red Provençal countryside. By three o'clock I was feeling tired, hungry and needed to go to the toilet. 'What shall we do about stopping?' I asked.

'Let's stop at the next service station,' she said. 'I need to get out of the car, too.' At the service station, I first filled the car with petrol, then went and parked the car in front of the shop. I went to the toilet. I was just washing my hands when a cleaner came in through another door, with a cheerful '*Bonjour, monsieur*'.

For some reason I looked out of the open door. It was at the back of the building. As I looked, a silver

Mercedes drove along the road from the car park. I was sure it was Andrea's car, although I couldn't see the number plate or the driver.

I went into the shop. When I looked through the big window I could see Sandra standing next to our car. She was talking fast Italian to someone on her mobile phone. I bought some orange juice and mineral water and went out to where the car was standing. Sandra was waiting by the car.

'Who were you talking to?' I asked.

She looked annoyed. Didn't she want me to know that she had been talking to someone?

'What's the matter with you, Paul?' she asked. 'You are suspicious of everything and everyone. I was just talking to my father, actually, to tell him that I was all right. He worries about me.'

'I see,' I said. But now I didn't really believe her, I couldn't believe her now, not after I thought I'd seen Andrea's Mercedes.

We drove on all afternoon. She was angry with me, but even that made me suspicious: why should she be angry if she had nothing to hide? She had the map-book open on her knees. Our only conversations were about directions and roads. Sandra's mobile phone rang three times and she answered in monosyllables – '*Sì*' and '*No*' and '*Ciao*' – which told me nothing.

I kept looking ahead and in my mirror to see if Andrea's silver car was anywhere, but it never was. But as time went on I did have an idea that we were being followed, at a distance. There was a yellow Fiat sports car that I often noticed several cars behind us. It could go much faster than my little Metro, and I couldn't understand why it just sat there behind us. And then I remembered that there had been a yellow Fiat exactly like that one in the car park when I had arrived at the Portofino villa.

On and on we went in the hot French summer sun. The red southern earth turned into rock and then into greener hill country, and as darkness fell we were getting near Clermont-Ferrand.

'I'm getting tired,' I said, breaking a long, long silence in which I'd had nothing but my own thoughts to play with. 'And hungry.'

'OK,' said Sandra. 'Let's find somewhere for the night.'

Chapter 10
An unhappy drive

Half an hour later I was parking the car in front of the Hotel de la Poste in the village of Issoire. I got out of the car and looked around. I couldn't see the silver Mercedes or the yellow Fiat. But that didn't mean anything. Inside, Sandra checked us in with the hotel receptionist in excellent French, and we went upstairs to our second-floor room.

'I'm just going out for a minute,' said Sandra. She left immediately. I lay down on the bed, feeling too tired to ask why and where. Half an hour later she reappeared. 'Right,' she said brightly. 'It's time for dinner. I've found a lovely little restaurant just across the square, and I've booked us a table for half an hour's time. Are you still hungry?'

'I could eat a horse!' I said, standing up. I walked to where she was and put my arms round her.

'Let's be friends, Sandra. I hate these long silences between us.'

'I want to be friends,' she said. 'But you keep saying terrible things about me ...'

'I'm sorry,' I said. 'But you must see how difficult it is for me to understand what's happening.'

'There's really nothing to understand, Paul,' she answered simply. 'Let's just enjoy our holiday.'

We kissed. A long deep kiss. Our first that day. It felt very good. I couldn't help myself.

After a very good dinner in the restaurant, I had a long shower and then fell into bed. I was very tired after my day of driving and I was asleep as soon as my head touched the pillow. I had the feeling that Sandra left the room and came back while I was asleep, but I have no idea what she did.

* * *

At six thirty the next morning Sandra, already fully dressed and made-up, woke me.

'There's *café au lait* and croissants on the table over there,' she said in a cold voice. 'I'd like to leave at seven if that's all right with you.'

Then she went out again. I got out of bed with difficulty. My body hurt after driving the day before. I had a quick cool shower to wake myself up. I dressed and while I was drinking coffee and eating a croissant

Sandra kept walking into the room, looking out of the window, then walking out again.

Looking out of the window down onto the square a few minutes later, I was just in time to see a silver Mercedes with Swiss number plates turn the corner and drive out of view. So Andrea really was around, I thought. Once again.

I wondered how I was going to find out what was happening – it was difficult to ask Sandra directly. I looked around the room to check that I'd left nothing behind and suddenly noticed Sandra's mobile telephone lying next to her coat on the chair.

I had an idea. I picked up the phone, went into the bathroom and dropped it inside the toilet. Then I heard the door open. I washed my hands, and walked back into the bedroom. Perhaps it was a silly thing to do, but I was fed up with her talking on the mobile phone.

'Your driver is ready, madam,' I said to Sandra, trying to make a joke. I picked up the two cases. She laughed – which was lovely to hear – and we left the hotel.

We drove out of the village with its dark stone buildings, past the pretty church which I'd visited with Jacky. That seemed such a long time ago now. We stopped for petrol on the edge of the village and soon were back on the E11 motorway driving north.

We had passed Clermont-Ferrand and were getting close to Bourges. Nothing had happened. The traffic was normal. I drove easily. The weather was cloudy but dry, and there was no sign of the other two cars. And Sandra had not yet noticed that her mobile phone was missing. We said nothing of importance. I sometimes asked for water from the bottles which she had bought in the morning. She also gave me apples and chocolate at regular intervals.

As I drove I thought about everything that had happened on the journey so far. Sandra's nervousness at the French border, the two cars that seemed to be following us, the way that Sandra went out of the hotel room several times, the phone-calls she kept receiving ...

I knew I had to find out what was really going on quickly, before we got to England. I felt happy that the mobile phone had now gone. That made it difficult for Sandra to call Andrea or anyone, and gave me more of a chance of finding out the truth.

Suddenly there was a scream. Sandra was pulling things out of her handbag, turning to search the pockets of her coat on the back seat, looking through the maps in the door pocket and feeling under her seat.

'Shit!' she shouted, and banged her hands on the map on her knee.

'What's the matter?' I asked, trying to sound worried and innocent at the same time.

'I can't find my phone,' she screamed, searching violently in her bag again.

'Calm down,' I said. 'It must be somewhere around. Take your time and have a good look.'

She tried again, but (of course!) it was useless.

'I don't suppose you know anything about it, do you?' she asked, turning to look at me.

'It's your phone, Sandra. You always have it with you. I haven't seen it,' I replied.

She put the things back into her handbag, crossed her arms across her chest and stared, hard-faced, at the endless motorway in front of her.

Chapter 11
A story is told

At around one o'clock we reached Paris. Sandra didn't want to go through the city, so we drove around the eastern side of the capital. I was starting to make a plan in my head. I realised I had more chance of finding out what was happening on the ordinary roads we were now using than on the motorway. There were traffic lights, people and police stations. Something would happen to help me. If a chance roof-tile could put me into this situation then something else unlikely could happen to get me out of it.

Why did I believe that some unexpected opportunity would arrive to help me? I have no idea. But it did. The cloudy sky, which had been getting darker the further north we got, turned to rain. At first the rain was light, but soon it was heavy enough for me to slow the car right down. I put the windscreen wipers at double speed and water from heavy lorries, driving out of Paris, was pushed hard against my small car.

And soon it became so dark, with thunder and lightning all around us, that I was driving along at less than twenty kilometres per hour.

Through the rain my headlights lit up a sign for a crossroads with the names of several small villages on it. I knew that soon we would be back onto main roads. I had to do something now. I thought that it would be difficult for Andrea and the others to follow us along small country lanes, so I decided to take a chance.

I checked behind me for headlights. There were some in the distance. I could see no more than fifty metres ahead. As we got closer to the crossroads I suddenly turned the steering wheel and drove quickly across the road and down a country lane. There was a loud sound of a horn and flashing of lights as a big lorry went past just behind us, but I'd done it. Sandra was thrown around by the violent and unexpected turn.

'Are you mad?' she screamed when she recovered. 'You nearly got us killed! Get back onto the other road at once!'

'No,' I said, very calmly and quietly.

'Get back this minute!' she shouted. 'Or I'll ... Or I'll ...'

'Or you'll what?' I asked. There was no answer. It was still pouring with rain. I drove the car for a few kilometres to make sure no-one was following us. Then I stopped the car by the side of the road. I had no idea what to do next. The only thought I had was that Sandra must have planned a meeting with Andrea for that evening.

I thought that Sandra's 'friends' would now be worried and suspicious because they hadn't been able to talk to her on her mobile phone. And they would almost certainly be very angry. But I suddenly realised that if there was something in my car that Andrea and Mr Rovello wanted to get to England, I was the key to the success of the operation. For some reason none of them could make the trip to England themselves – they needed someone else to do it. Perhaps they already had criminal records.

'So,' said Sandra once we had stopped moving, 'What are we going to do now?'

'You think about it,' I said, and pushing the seat back, I closed my eyes. Soon I could hear the sound of Sandra crying. At first I tried to ignore her but then I couldn't stand it any more. I turned to her.

'Sandra, what's the matter?' I asked, touching her arm. She pushed me off.

'Leave me alone. You've caused nothing but problems all along.'

It was difficult to understand her through the hand that covered her face and through the tears.

'Hey, come on!' I replied. 'It's you who's behaving strangely, not me.'

At this she started crying even more.

'It's not me,' she said with difficulty. 'They make me do these things.'

'What do you mean?' I asked, totally confused by what she had just said and wanting to hear more. Slowly she tried to stop crying. She blew her nose. She looked a mess. Her eyes and face were red and her make-up was in black lines around her cheeks. She looked like a little lost girl and I suddenly felt very sorry for her.

'Can you tell me?' I asked very gently, reaching for her hand and holding it to give her strength.

In a very quiet voice she started to talk.

'It's very difficult to explain, Paul, but you know some things already, and I want to show you that I didn't want to do any of this. It's him.'

'It's who?' I asked.

'Andrea,' she answered, starting to cry again. As soon as she was able to, she continued.

'My father was a successful businessman. He had a small company with those two other men you saw in

Portofino as partners. They were involved in the import and export of reproduction furniture, furniture that looks like antiques. They had business connections all over the world, but especially in England and France. It was a good business for a long time, but about ten years ago, things started to get difficult.'

'But where does Andrea come in?' I asked, taking hold of her hand again.

'Business was so slow that my father and his partners owed a lot of money and they thought they might have to close their business down. Then they met Andrea. He had very good connections in America where the reproduction furniture business was still good. It seemed that Andrea could help the company, so my father and his partners decided to let him try.'

'And were they successful?' I asked.

'Very,' Sandra answered. 'In fact they were so successful that at the end of the first year my father and his partners made Andrea a partner, too. Everyone was happy – it seemed as if everything was going to be all right. Andrea was very sweet to our family at first, and especially to me. And I thought he was very nice.'

'He's a lot older than you, isn't he?' I said.

'Yes, Paul, he is ... but we started a relationship. My parents were very happy about it. The family is still very important for Italians. They felt that Andrea had saved them. He was part of the business, and some time in the future, they thought, he might be part of the family. Everything would be safe for me. And I loved him ... At least, I did at first ...'

She stopped and looked down, a painful expression on her face. I gave her a light kiss on her cheek, then she went on. 'Soon, however, my father started to get very worried about what was happening in the business. More furniture was going and coming from America than in the first year, but the profits were much bigger. My father couldn't understand it. The new customers seemed to be paying a lot more for the furniture than the companies he had worked with before.

'Of course we all enjoyed the increased profits. We all had the car we wanted. My father bought Villa Bellavista and forgot about Magreglio. My mother was able to fill the house with the glass and paintings she had always wanted. Everyone was happy. On the surface. But underneath my father knew something wasn't right.

'In the end, about two years later, he and the other two partners asked Andrea to explain what was happening, and the truth came out. He started off buying and selling reproduction furniture for the company, but then he started to change the reproduction furniture for real antique chairs and cupboards. These antiques were mostly stolen, but customs authorities thought it was just reproduction furniture. He was taking large amounts of very valuable antique Italian furniture into America. It was very clever, but it was clear that he was just using my father's company. He was also bringing back all kinds of works of art from there.'

'My God!' I shouted. 'But why didn't your father report Andrea to the police?'

'He couldn't,' she replied very simply. 'Don't you see that my father and his partners were in it too? They were the owners of the company, and they had enjoyed the profits of this illegal business. Even I was a small part of it. I had my car, my clothes, my exciting holidays, and my regular trips across the border into Switzerland to take things ...'

'What things?' I said, wanting to know exactly what I'd had in the car that day.

'Oh, antique jewellery usually – I'd been stopped at the border the time before I asked you to drive to

Lugano. Fortunately I'd had nothing on me. But that's why Andrea told me to ask you to take me there in your car. You were not suspicious to the customs authorities, and we needed to get it there quickly. It was for a very important customer.'

'But surely if you'd explained everything to the police they would have understood,' I started.

'Oh, Paul, it's not so simple,' she said loudly. 'Don't you understand that we are all in Andrea's power, even though my father still looks as if he runs the company? All of us would go to prison if anyone had said anything.'

'And so it was Andrea's idea to get me to drive you to England with the ... the ... whatever it is we've got in this car?' I asked.

'Well, I really wanted to go there with you on holiday,' she replied, looking at me nervously. 'But something went wrong in the United States two weeks ago and Andrea said we would have to take something with us ... and, oh Paul, I didn't want to get you involved. I really didn't. You must believe me!'

'Why are they following us now?' I asked.

'They want to make sure that the operation is successful. When we found out the truth about Andrea I finished our relationship, so he doesn't trust me completely.'

I knew now what one of the bodyguards was doing with my car at four o'clock in the morning at Portofino. I had one more question. 'What is in my car? What have they put in my car?'

'I don't know. Probably paintings that they want to get out of the country.'

I looked at Sandra. I could see she was telling the truth and a warm feeling went through my body.

'Oh, Sandra!' I said softly, putting my arms around her and pulling her close to me. 'I believe you. I thought it was you who had been using me all this time.'

She let me hold her close to me, and I felt her start crying again. I held her quietly for what seemed like a long time. Finally she sat up, cleared her eyes, and looked at me.

'No, Paul. Not at all. Never!' she said. 'I didn't want to get you involved in any of the mess that my family is in. But Andrea says that he will tell the police and my family will all end up in prison because everything is in my father's name.' And here the tears came again, and she cried and cried in my arms.

Chapter 12
A bad morning

We sat in that old car of mine on the side of the road and held each other silently for a very long time. Then we started to talk. We decided that the best thing to do would be to return to Italy. We would return to Italy and meet Sandra's father somewhere where Andrea couldn't find us. We would phone Mr Rovello as soon as we could to explain what had happened and arrange a meeting place. We thought it was best to try and persuade him to go to the Italian police and explain the whole situation. We felt the police would understand the Rovello family's problems. After all, it was Andrea who did the illegal business.

The rain had stopped, but it was getting dark when we stopped in front of a small hotel at Chateaudon, a hundred kilometres south. It had taken us longer to travel back because we had decided to stay off the motorways in case Andrea and his friends were looking for us.

After a shower and change of clothes, we ate the usual excellent French hotel dinner in the restaurant downstairs. It was a quiet meal. We were both very tired, and each of us felt very pleased in our own way. Sandra had told me the truth and didn't have to hide what was happening from me any more. And I finally understood much of the story which I had been involved in. Of course, we were both still worried about the next part. Many difficult problems lay ahead, not least getting back to Italy safely. After a couple of glasses of Calvados in the small bar, we went to bed early. We slept closely together all night, feeling the new warmth of being on the same side.

* * *

At about six thirty the next morning we were woken by loud knocking on the bedroom door. Sandra got out of bed with difficulty and went across to the door.

'Wait, Sandra ...' I shouted, waking up a bit, 'Find out who ...'

It was too late. At that moment she turned the key and the door opened. Sandra was pushed across the room onto the bed by Andrea. One of the guards I'd seen in Portofino followed him in, locking the door behind him. They were both holding guns.

Sandra moved close to me on the bed, and I put my arm around her. She was shaking with fear and her face was very white. The two men stood at the foot of the bed, staring at us and looking dangerous.

'So,' said Andrea slowly, with a horrible smile on his face, 'we have found our runaway lovers.'

He and the other man looked at each other and laughed.

'But how ... ?' I started.

'You stupid Englishman!' shouted the big man. 'Do you imagine we would have let you go driving around Europe with a car containing a number of priceless ...'

'Careful!' cut in Andrea. 'A car containing some very valuable things, without keeping a close check on where you were? We are not stupid, Mr Morris! I put a very strong radio signal on your car in Portofino so that we could always find you. And here you are!' said Andrea, with a cold laugh.

Sandra turned to me with an 'I didn't know anything about it' look on her face, and I took her hand to show that I believed her.

'Now get dressed and packed and be ready in twenty minutes!' ordered Andrea. 'Take out the telephone.'

The big guard pulled the telephone off the wall. Then they both left, locking the bedroom door behind them. I pulled Sandra closer to me, and we held each other for a few moments.

'What shall we do now?' she asked, standing up.

'I have no idea at present,' I answered, still surprised that they'd been able to find us so easily, and angry with myself for not having thought that they would have checked our movements closely. As they said, whatever was in the car was far too valuable ('priceless' was the guard's word) to leave to chance. Once again I wondered what it could be. I got out of bed and walked over to my suitcase.

'Well, I think we'd better do as they ask,' said Sandra. 'We can make a plan as we go along. And Paul ...'

'Yes?' I turned to face her, and she walked over to where I was standing. 'I really didn't know anything about the radio signal in the car,' she said.

'I know you didn't,' I replied, giving her a smile, and stretching out my hands to her. She took my hands in hers and stood looking at me. 'And anyway, there's something I want to tell you.'

'Yes?' she said with an uncertain look on her face.

'Sandra, I love you,' I said, and then added: 'And when all this is over I want to be with you all the time. I ... I ... I want to marry you.'

I must say that I hadn't really thought about marriage, but I'd realised after her explanation yesterday that I really did love her. I'd been so uncertain about my feelings, confused as they had been at first with Jacky's death and then with this awful nightmare. And now it seemed as if a window had been opened in a dark room, and sunlight was coming in so that I could understand everything.

'Oh, Paul,' she said, staring at me almost in disbelief. 'How can you love me when all I've done is bring you so much trouble? And when we don't even know how we're going to get out of this?'

'I know it looks impossible at present,' I replied, pulling her closer to me, 'but we'll be all right. Just tell me one thing: do you love me?'

'I do, Paul, I do. It just seems so difficult now ...' She stopped speaking and tears came to her eyes. I put my hands on either side of her face, and looked into her eyes.

'No crying now, my love,' I said softly. 'I need all your help now. OK?'

She nodded, and smiled. I gave her a kiss on her pretty lips.

'Come on,' I said. 'Let's get ready.'

* * *

Twenty minutes later we were let out of the room by the guard and taken downstairs to the car park where Andrea was waiting for us. Their cars were parked on either side of mine.

'Now listen very carefully,' Andrea started in an unpleasant voice, pointing at me. 'You've already given us enough problems. And this new delay means that we will have to wait a day or two here in France.'

'Why?' asked Sandra.

'Because our connections in England tell us that the customs authorities at the border will be checking everyone who goes into the country. Apparently, they are looking for some international terrorist group. If we had got in this morning it would have been all right, but now we are too late. Because of your boyfriend.'

'So what are we going to do?' I asked.

'We're going to have a little holiday, Mr Morris, at the French seaside,' answered Andrea. 'We are going to drive to Dieppe and wait until you can cross the Channel to Newhaven. It's about 250 kilometres to Dieppe from here. We can easily get there by lunchtime. We will all go together. Alessandra – you will go in my car so you don't get any more clever ideas about running away. Mr Morris – you will follow our guard here. His yellow car is very easy to see, so you will not make any mistakes. Do you understand? After all, you would not like anything to happen to Alessandra, would you?'

'What do you mean?' I asked.

'I don't think I need to explain,' said Andrea, pushing Sandra towards his Mercedes. 'Just do as you have been told and everything will be all right.'

Chapter 13 The farmhouse

I did as I was told. I drove along the main roads northwards between the two cars. Whenever I looked in the mirror I could see Sandra sitting beside Andrea in the front seat of the silver Mercedes, as she must have done many times before.

I felt very alone. I had no idea what to do, especially now that I was not with Sandra any more. It seemed to take away my ability to think and act. And anyway, after what Andrea had said, I was afraid of what they might do to her if I tried to escape. So I drove along in a kind of dream.

* * *

The towns came and went. The roads were dry, the traffic was not too busy and by half past eleven we were driving into the suburbs of Dieppe. There, the guard signalled and stopped at the roadside; I stopped behind him, and Andrea came up and parked right behind me. The guard and Andrea got out and had a discussion with a map opened on the roof of the guard's car. I turned round and smiled to Sandra, and she blew me a kiss back.

Once the two men had decided where to go, they got back into their cars and we started again. I followed the yellow Fiat sports car into the town centre, then out along a coast road until we came to a lonely old farmhouse near the sea. The guard turned into the drive and then into a car park behind the farmhouse. I followed. Andrea and Sandra drove past the house. I wondered where they had gone to, but soon realised that they had been to collect the keys.

'Right, you,' said the guard, when they had returned, 'get out of the car, get your bags and follow me.' I did as I was told. We were let into the house through the back door by Andrea.

'Car keys,' ordered the big guard, stretching out his hand. I gave them to him.

'Don't forget to take his passport too,' said Andrea. 'I've already got Alessandra's.'

'Upstairs, both of you,' said the guard.

We were taken upstairs and put in different rooms at the back of the house. The doors were locked.

'Please,' I heard Sandra shouting, 'I need to go to the bathroom, and I'm hungry and thirsty, too.'

'Wait,' came the answer. I could hear Andrea and the guard talking below, but it was impossible to understand what they were saying. Some time later the door opened and closed with a bang, and I heard the yellow Fiat starting. Looking out of the window, I saw it drive off.

It returned about half an hour later, and soon footsteps came up the stairs. Sandra's door was opened and she was allowed to go to the bathroom, before being locked in again. Then it was my turn. Before being locked in again, I was given two large bottles of mineral water, some French bread, some Camembert cheese and two bars of chocolate. I sat down on the bed and ate.

When I'd finished I started to examine the room carefully. It was simply furnished – a bed, a table and chair, a wardrobe and a colourful carpet in the middle. There was one window which looked out onto the car park, the untidy garden behind, and across some fields. The sea was in the opposite direction. I wondered what to do next. I was a prisoner. I needed to escape. But how?

I walked to the window and tried to open it. It was impossible. I walked over to the door. It was quite thick, and well locked. What else could I do? The walls? I put my ear against the wall between my room and Sandra's room, hoping I could hear something. I couldn't. I knocked on the wall and waited. Nothing. I knocked harder and waited. There was an answering knock.

Knock, knock, I went. Knock, knock, she went.

'Hello,' I said. Nothing. Obviously it was a thick wall. There was no way out of the room. Disappointed, I lay down on the bed on my back with my hands behind my head staring up at the ceiling. The ceiling! There in the middle of the ceiling was a door which went up into the roof.

I lay there for a while looking at the small door in the ceiling, wondering how I was going to get up to it. It was about three and a half metres from the floor. I sat up and looked around the room. I moved the chair from under the table, and with no noise I picked up the table itself, and carried it across the room until it was underneath the door in the ceiling. I put the chair next to it and climbed up on the table. The ceiling was just above my head now, and I put my arms up and pushed the painted wooden door. It stayed shut. I pushed again, harder this time, and there was a small movement. I kept pushing.

Suddenly, the door moved upwards with a rather loud noise. I stood still and listened, hoping that the two men downstairs had heard nothing. As there was no sudden running of feet on the stairs, I guessed I had been lucky. Next I pulled the chair up onto the table and carefully climbed up on it. I pushed the wooden door to one side and put my head and shoulders through the hole and looked into the space below the roof.

I had no idea what to expect, but I was surprised by what I saw. The roof was very high and there were two windows through which sunlight came, lighting the whole central area. There were some boxes at one end, and lots of old farm things. This had probably been a space to keep things when the building was a farmhouse. There was probably a door to the outside somewhere through which things would be pulled up from below.

I looked around carefully. Above the window of my room I could see three lines of light in the wall. They were in the shape of a double door. I was just going to get up into the roof, when I heard a noise from below. Quickly, I put the door back over the opening, but I couldn't make it fall back into place! There was no time now, as the footsteps were at the top of the stairs. I climbed down from the chair and off the table, then put the chair back onto the floor.

I heard a knock on Sandra's door, and the guard's voice asking in Italian if she wanted anything. Sandra said something, the lock was turned and she was allowed to go to the bathroom again.

While this was happening I replaced the table and chair in their positions. As I lay down on the bed, the key was turned in the lock of the door and the big guard walked in.

I looked across at him, hoping he wouldn't look up at the ceiling where there were dirty marks by the door.

'Do you want anything?' he asked roughly.

'Yes, I'd like to go to the bathroom, please.'

I went over to my case and took out my wash-bag and a towel, and walked out to the bathroom. I looked at my face in the mirror. I was a mess. I hadn't shaved in the morning, I had dirt on my face from the roof and lines under my eyes from having little sleep and worrying a lot. I washed and shaved and felt better. The guard was sitting on a chair in the corridor when I came out. As I passed Sandra's room I knocked on the door.

'Sandra,' I shouted. 'Are you all right?'

'Paul,' came her voice. 'Yes, I'm fine. What about you? What's happening?'

'I'm OK,' I replied. 'I don't know what's going on. I suppose we're just waiting until we can cross to England. I don't know if – '

'All right,' said the guard, walking up to me. 'That's enough. Get back in your room.'

I did as I was told. The door was locked behind me again, and the guard's footsteps disappeared downstairs. I looked at my watch – it was five o'clock. I decided not to get up in the roof now. I would wait until Andrea and the guard had gone to bed. I ate some more bread, cheese and chocolate. At ten o'clock there was another visit from the guard to let me go to the bathroom. I said goodnight to Sandra through the door.

Chapter 14 Escape

Back in my room, I looked through my case and decided what things I would take with me. I changed into dark clothes so that I would not be seen so easily at night. Then I set my alarm clock for one o'clock in the morning, got into bed fully dressed and switched off the light. It was a good thing I did so. At around midnight, I heard footsteps coming upstairs. My door was unlocked, the light was switched on for a second as either Andrea or the guard checked on me.

After that I lay in the dark, waiting. I must have fallen asleep because I woke up suddenly when the alarm went off at one o'clock. I sat up in the dark, listening. It was very quiet. I could hear the noise of the sea outside. I got out of bed and repeated my actions of the afternoon with the table and chair. Then I tied my trainers together, and put them round my neck. I'd be much quieter in just my socks, I thought.

Soon I was pulling myself up into the space under the roof. The floor made a noise as I stood up. Moonlight came in through the windows, giving me a little light. I stood still for a minute letting my eyes get used to things. Then I walked slowly and softly across to the double doors. I couldn't see how they opened in the afternoon. I would have to do it all by touch now in the dark. I found the door, and moved my hands up and down it. There was no lock and key in the middle, so I moved down to the bottom. There was something metal there. I felt and turned it, and pulled upwards. Nothing happened. I put both hands on it and pulled hard up. The door moved suddenly, and I fell over backwards with a noise onto the floor.

I lay there for a minute or two breathing fast after the effort. I listened hard to see if the noise had woken anyone. Silence. I stood up and pushed the door. It swung open with a horrible noise – it must have been shut for years. I waited again.

There was still no sound from inside the house. I looked down. It was, I suppose, about six or seven metres to the ground. I hadn't thought about how I would get down. I walked quietly around, looking to see if I could find a rope or a ladder or something else to help. There was nothing. I went over to the door and looked down again. I suppose I'll have to jump, I thought. But I didn't like the idea of jumping down onto the hard ground.

I put on my trainers, then I sat on the edge of the roof door. It was a long way down! I waited for a moment and then dropped down and then rolled over as I hit the ground. I stood up and brushed myself down. I walked over to my car. The doors and boot were all locked.

I sat down beside the car in the dark. I quickly thought through what I needed to do and made a list in my mind: one, get back into the house; two, find my car keys and, if possible, our passports; three, get Sandra; four, leave. It didn't sound very easy!

I took a deep breath and walked to the back door of the house. To my surprise it was open. I walked in, leaving the door open behind me for a quick escape if necessary. I stood and listened. But I couldn't hear anything. I took my trainers off, putting them round my neck again. It was very dark in the house, and I wondered if I could turn on the light to look for the keys.

Suddenly there was a noise upstairs. A door opened, and I heard footsteps go along the corridor. I stood very still. The bathroom door opened and shut. I moved quickly out of the hall and into the living room where the moonlight through the windows showed me a large sofa. I got down behind it. I heard the toilet, then a light was turned on, and footsteps came down the stairs. I felt cold sweat running down my back as they came closer. The light in the living room was switched on, and someone walked across and went into the kitchen. I heard the outside door shut.

I looked out from behind the sofa, checking the

room. Table and chairs, a fireplace, two armchairs, a large clock showing one thirty, a cupboard, a TV, a bookshelf ... My eyes went back to the cupboard. I thought I could see some keys and papers on it.

At that moment there was a noise from the kitchen, and someone came out. I got down behind the sofa again. The light went off, and the footsteps went back upstairs. I hoped that he wouldn't check my room. He didn't.

I stayed behind the sofa for what seemed like an hour, but was in fact only about ten minutes. When it seemed safe to move, I walked quietly across to the cupboard and felt for the keys and papers I'd seen when the light was on. I picked them up and moved over to the window, and looked at them in the moonlight.

I was surprised to find that there were two sets of keys. One of them was my car keys, and the other looked like the house keys. I was even more surprised to find both of our passports were there, too. I put everything into my pocket. Now for Sandra, I thought.

Out in the hall I stood in the darkness, listening. I could hear nothing from upstairs. I started to move up the stairs as slowly as possible. I waited after each movement. My heart was beating loudly. Finally, I reached the top of the stairs and moved gently along to Sandra's room. I turned the key in the lock as slowly as I could, pushed the door open, moved inside and closed the door behind me. I turned the light on. Sandra sat up in bed, with her hands over her eyes.

'*Ma, che cosa ...?*' she said, dangerously loudly. I put my finger on my lips, and she saw it was me. I walked over to her bed and sat down beside her. We held each other for a moment.

'But how ...?' she started again.

'It doesn't matter now,' I whispered. 'Get dressed and put what you want into your handbag as quickly as you can. We're leaving. And don't put your shoes on.'

She did as I asked. When she was ready, I turned the light off, and we went out into the corridor. I listened for a moment. Then I locked the door and took the key out of her door and mine – anything that might buy us time later!

We moved slowly, nervously, downstairs – any noise might bring the guard or Andrea running with their guns, and our escape would be over. Once down in the kitchen we both put our shoes on and went outside. I took the house keys out of my pocket and locked the door behind me, and then I threw the keys away.

'We'll push the car down to the road,' I said to Sandra, as I opened the doors, 'so that when I start the engine it won't be so close to the house.'

Sandra agreed. We pushed the car out from between the other two cars.

'Thank goodness it's such a small car!' whispered Sandra across the roof. Gently we pushed the car out onto the road. Suddenly Sandra turned and ran back down the path and disappeared. I was alone in the dark. What was she doing? Had she decided to return to Andrea? Was she going to give me up? I was suddenly suspicious of her again. Any minute I thought a light would go on and someone would start shooting at me. I was about to get into the car when I saw Sandra coming back.

'What did you do? Where did you ...?' I asked.

'Quickly,' she said. 'Get into the car.'

We pushed the car a bit more and jumped in. The car hit something and my door shut very loudly. I tried to start the car. Nothing happened. It wouldn't start. We stared at each other. We were both frightened. I looked back at the house and tried to start the car again. Nothing.

A light went on and a window opened in one of the front bedrooms. A head appeared shouting something in Italian. I tried to start the car again.

'Come on!' I whispered to the car, trying a fourth time. This time it started. Just then there was a loud bang from the house and a noise at the back of the car.

'Quick!' shouted Sandra. 'They're shooting at us!'

There was another bang, and a noise on the roof of the car this time.

'Keep your head down,' I said. I kept the car headlights off until we turned the first corner. Then I put them on and drove off as fast as I could. There were more shots as we went down the road, but none of them hit the car.

Chapter 15
South across France

'What were you doing back there?' I shouted at Sandra. 'What were you doing? We could have been caught. They'll catch us very quickly now.' I was angry with Sandra – although, if I think about it, it was my door that shut loudly and woke them up.

In fact Sandra had saved us some time. 'I was cutting their tyres,' she said, and held up a knife.

'How did you get that?' I asked, feeling happier now.

'The guard lent it to me last night to cut up my bread and cheese,' she answered. 'I cut all four tyres on both cars, so they'll have to get them changed. I guess that gives us a couple of hours, even if they can get someone to come out and change them at this time of night.'

'You're absolutely amazing, Sandra Rovello!' I shouted.

I hadn't thought about where we should go. As

we drove towards Dieppe, I asked Sandra what she thought.

'I think we still need to get back to Italy,' she said.

'OK. Italy, here we come.'

We drove south, stopping to fill up with petrol and buy something to eat and drink at the first petrol station out of the city. It was five o'clock in the morning. We were very tired but we thought we should still keep driving. Sandra slept a little and, at about one o'clock in the afternoon, we stopped again. We needed more petrol, and we needed to rest. After filling up the car with petrol and having a drink in the bar, Sandra telephoned her father to tell him what had happened. We arranged to meet at the Italian border the next day. We then moved the car over to the corner of the car park to have a rest.

'Let's rest for an hour and then we'll continue.'

I pushed the driver's seat back and was so tired I quickly fell asleep.

* * *

I awoke suddenly. Sandra was asleep beside me. I looked at my watch. 'Bloody hell!' I shouted. 'Sandra. Sandra. Wake up quickly. It's four o'clock!' She awoke with difficulty.

'What?' she said. 'What's the matter?'

'Quickly. Let's get going. It's four o'clock. We've slept too long!' I shouted.

We got ourselves ready and left at once.

'We're both exhausted after sleeping so little and having so many things to worry about,' I said to Sandra as we were driving. 'We'll be fine. I'm sure cutting their tyres bought us the sleeping time we needed. Now we can drive straight to the border.'

Chapter 16
A motorway chase

But we'd forgotten about the radio signal that Andrea had put on the car. We had been driving south for about twenty minutes, with the pretty line of the Mâconnais wine hills on our right side, when I saw something yellow in the distance in my mirror. As it got closer, I realised it was a yellow Fiat sports car. I had a sick feeling in my stomach.

'Sandra,' I said very quietly. 'Look behind us.'

She turned around. 'Oh no!' she said. 'But how could he have found us already?'

'Well, don't forget that his car can go about twice as fast as mine,' I answered. 'And he can also follow us with the radio signal.'

'And there's Andrea, too!' she suddenly shouted. 'Look! Behind that Belgian lorry.'

I looked in the mirror. There was the silver Mercedes just overtaking a big lorry. My heart almost stopped. What could we do now? Then I had an idea.

'Show me the map, Sandra,' I said quickly. She turned it round, and put her finger on Dijon so I could see where we were more easily.

'Right. We're not going to leave the motorway now, as planned. We're going to keep on going south on the A6 towards Lyon.'

'But why should we do that?' she asked, confused. 'Both their cars are much faster than ours.'

'That's just the point,' I explained. 'If we leave the motorway the road becomes very hilly, and this little car can't go up hills very well, so it would be very easy for them to catch us. Also, it's a much quieter road, with less police and help on it. What I'm going to do is drive as fast as I can along this flat motorway. They'll have to follow. Hopefully the police will soon notice all of these cars driving too fast. Once we see the police are following, we'll stop and you'll explain everything in your beautiful French. It's our only chance now, Sandra. Otherwise Andrea will just stop us and do what he wants.'

'But, Paul, that's very dangerous,' she said, with a worried look in her eyes.

'But it's no more dangerous than being caught by Andrea and that big guard, is it?' I asked.

'No, I suppose not,' she answered. 'But be careful, Paul.'

I kissed her cheek. Looking in the mirror I could see the guard's yellow Fiat two cars back and Andrea's Mercedes about another four cars back. I was in the middle lane, and the traffic was quite light.

'Right,' I said. 'Here we go.'

I went faster and faster. I'd never really wanted to see how fast the Metro could go – it said 180 kph on the speedometer, but I don't think I'd ever gone faster than 130 before. Soon I was driving at 170 in the fast lane of the motorway. I had my headlights on and my warning lights flashing.

'I don't think you'd better go any faster,' shouted Sandra nervously over the noise of the engine. The car obviously didn't like this very much.

'No,' I shouted back. 'This is OK. They're following.'

Both cars had moved out to follow us and were a couple of hundred metres behind, with Andrea's Mercedes just in front of the yellow Fiat now.

'And look!' shouted Sandra, excitedly pointing upwards. 'There's a police car on the bridge ahead.' I flashed my headlights several times as we came up to the bridge, hoping to get their attention.

By now Andrea was close behind me, and flashing his lights, too. When Sandra looked round, he waved his arm and pointed over to the side of the road.

'He's signalling us to move over,' she said. 'He must be mad!'

'Can you see the guard?' I asked. I could only see Andrea in my mirror.

'Yes, he's a hundred metres or so behind Andrea. And ...' She took a deep breath. 'Paul, Paul ... there's a police car behind, too. I can see the blue lights. Your plan's working!'

I tried to make the Metro go even faster. Ahead of me there wasn't much traffic, and any cars in front moved over into the middle lane as I flashed my lights. We were doing over 180 now. The engine was making a terrible noise and the whole car was shaking. At the next junction, Sandra saw two more police cars join in the chase.

She looked at Andrea, who was no more than twenty metres behind us, and said some terrible things about him in Italian. He signalled again. A space opened up on the inside and I changed lane without slowing my speed. Andrea followed.

Then I moved into the emergency lane, still going as fast. The surface wasn't very good and there was a lot of tyre noise.

'Careful, Paul,' said Sandra in a loud, frightened voice, as she turned to face forward again. 'Look ahead!'

In the far distance I could see a large lorry in the emergency lane. It was getting closer very quickly.

'Oh my God!' I shouted, and started to slow down. Immediately there was a bang from behind, and my car was pushed violently. Sandra screamed and we both fell forward despite our seat-belts. Andrea had driven into the back of us when I slowed so suddenly. He had not seen what was happening ahead. I braked hard and fast, in a cloud of burning rubber and dust, but it was too late.

The Metro and I were not good enough to avoid hitting the lorry. The car turned right as it came to a stop, and the whole left-hand side of the car – Sandra's side – went hard into the back of the lorry. There was a terrible noise of metal against metal and a single long scream from Sandra. Then silence.

* * *

When I woke up I was lying in the back of an ambulance. I tried to sit up. I couldn't. There was a nurse there. The first thing I asked her was, 'Where's Sandra?' The serious-faced French nurse nodded her head. I fell unconscious again.

Chapter 17
Life now

I am sitting here now, looking out over this beautiful lake. The summer sun is going down, making long orange reflections across the water. I would like to say that, in a way, the sun went down on my life that day. There is much I could say, but I suppose I should tell you the rest of the story.

My car crashed into the back of the lorry. I had only a few small injuries, but Sandra's injuries were a bit more serious. She was in hospital for a few months and I spent most of my time by her bed.

After Andrea hit the back of my car he lost control of the Mercedes and crashed over the edge of the motorway and hit a tree. He died immediately. He was later recognised by the police as Andrea da Carta, also known as Andrew Card, and as Carter Andrews. He was known to Interpol and wanted for a number of big art robberies across Europe and America.

The guard was stopped by the French police for driving his yellow Fiat sports car too fast. They found out that he worked for Andrea, helping him to steal works of art and he was put in prison for ten years. When the house at Magreglio was searched later, a number of stolen paintings, sculptures and antique jewellery were found.

And when my car was searched carefully they found three internationally important paintings, stolen from Italy and the United States of America.

Sandra and I were allowed to go free, although the French police told me to drive more carefully in future. Later, in Italy, when all the information about Andrea and his business came out, the police agreed that Mr Rovello and his partners had been in a very difficult situation. Most of the stolen furniture and paintings were found and Mr Rovello returned to his reproduction furniture business.

As you may have guessed, Sandra and I married as soon as she was better. Unfortunately, it didn't last very long. Maybe we were just different types of people. Maybe it was the situation she and her family had got themselves into, maybe it was the terrible car accident in France ... Whatever it was, a space grew between us after the accident that seemed to grow bigger every day.

And so a year after our marriage we agreed to spend some months living apart to see if that would help. It didn't help very much, so we decided to divorce. About a year after that Sandra married a doctor, and they moved to America.

Once again I decided to stay in Como. As with Jacky's death, I felt that I wanted to stay in Italy. Italy was one of the things that Jacky loved and I still love. Or maybe it's because Italy reminds me of Jacky that I've stayed here. So I bought this lovely old house on the edge of Lake Como. Jacky would have loved it here ...

Now that I think of it, Jacky and I loved each other in a beautiful, innocent way ... I still miss that love, that innocent love, even after all these years ...

After the adventure with Sandra I continued to work for Corvo Pharmaceuticals. But soon after the divorce I started my own company. I run it from home using e-mail, the Internet, phone-calls and faxes.

These days I am mostly alone. In many ways my life has been very easy. And there has been plenty of time to think about how things work. I have thought about the relationship between humans and this earth we live on. And I have tried to understand how everything is a matter of chance ...

A roof-tile falls.

A roof-tile stays where it is.

After reading

读后活动

Choose some of these activities.

1. After reading *A Matter of Chance*, how important do you think chance has been in your life?
2. Would you like to live and work in a foreign country, like Paul and Jacky? Why or why not?
3. Which chapter from *A Matter of Chance* can you remember most clearly? Why?
4. Who are your favourite and least favourite characters in the story?
5. Paul gradually became suspicious of Sandra. Make a list of everything he noticed.
6. On Page 86, Sandra phoned her father to tell him what had happened. Try to write out the telephone conversation.
7. Make your own activities for other students to do, e.g. write some True/False questions.

Learning guide | 学习指导

Chapter 1

New words 生词

- instantly /ˈɪnstəntli/ *ad.* 立即
- roof-tile /ˈru:f-taɪl/ *n.* 屋顶瓦片

Reading exercises 阅读练习

1. Who is telling the story?
2. Which character is 'my wife'?

Chapter 2

New words 生词

- accommodation /əˌkɒməˈdeɪʃn/ *n.* 住宿；膳宿
- adventure /ədˈventʃə(r)/ *n.* 冒险
- airfare /ˈeəfeə(r)/ *n.* 机票钱；飞机票价
- application /ˌæplɪˈkeɪʃn/ *n.* 申请
- appointment /əˈpɔɪntmənt/ *n.*（报纸上的）招聘
- enlarge /ɪnˈlɑ:dʒ/ *v.* 扩大
- enthusiastic /ɪnˌθju:ziˈæstɪk/ *a.* 有激情的
- pharmaceuticals/ˌfɑ:məˈsu:tɪklz/ *n. pl.* 药品；制药厂
- section /ˈsekʃn/ *n.* 部分

- scenery /ˈsiːnəri/ *n.* 风景；景色
- well-established /ˈwel-ɪˈstæblɪʃt/ *a.* 得到确认的；固定下来的

Phrases & expressions 短语和表达

- evening class（成人参加的）夜校
- lead to ... 导致……
- knock down 撞倒
- photo album 相册
- step out 暂时外出；走出去

Cultural notes 文化点滴

- Como: 科莫。意大利北部阿尔卑斯山南麓城市，在科莫湖西南端，米兰以北 40 公里处。该市有建于 1215 年的市政厅、14 世纪的大理石教堂等哥特式与文艺复兴时期的建筑。
- Easter: 复活节。西方国家的一个重要节日，在每年春分月圆之后第一个星期日。
- Leonard Cohen: 莱纳德•科恩。1934 年出生于加拿大魁北克省，音乐家、作曲家、小说家、诗人。早年以诗歌和小说在文坛成名，其小说《美丽失落者》被评论家誉为 20 世纪 60 年代的经典之作。他一面以独特的乐风享誉世界，一面以诗歌与小说在严肃文学争得一席之地。2008 年，科恩获选进入美国摇滚名人堂；2009 年，获得格莱美终身成就奖。文中歌词来自他的歌曲 *Hey, That's No Way to Say Goodbye*。
- Manchester: 曼彻斯特。英国第二大城市，英国重要的交通枢纽与商业、金融、工业、文化中心。

Reading exercise 阅读练习

True or false?

_____ a) Paul often looks at his wife's photographs.

_____ b) Paul and Jacky met at work in Manchester.

_____ c) Paul and Jacky were engaged for two years.

_____ d) Jacky could speak excellent Italian.

_____ e) Paul and Jacky's friends thought it was a good idea to go to Italy.

Chapter 3

New words 生词

- despite /dɪˈspaɪt/ *prep.* 尽管
- exhausted /ɪɡˈzɔːstɪd/ *a.* 筋疲力尽的
- guilty /ˈɡɪlti/ *a.* 愧疚的
- perfume /ˈpɜːfjuːm/ *n.* 香水；香味
- picture /ˈpɪktʃə(r)/ *v.* 构想
- properly /ˈprɒpəli/ *ad.* 正确地，适宜地
- suppose /səˈpəʊz/ *v.* 认为；假设

Phrases & expressions 短语和表达

- fill in ... 填写……
- fill up ... 填补……
- in return 回敬；作为回报
- let go of ... 放开……
- take over 接手

Cultural note 文化点滴

- Veneto: 威尼托大区。位于意大利东北部，是意大利 20 个一级行政区之一，首府是“水城”威尼斯。该区还有世界文化遗产名录中的“帕拉迪奥之城”维琴察、传说中罗密欧与朱丽叶的故乡维罗纳，以及拥有全世界最古老大学之一的“大学者的城市”帕多瓦。

Reading exercise 阅读练习

Put the events in the right order.

_____ a) Paul realised he needed a change in his life.

_____ b) Paul's work became his life.

_____ c) Paul thought about a relationship with Sandra.

_____ d) After Jacky's death, Paul stayed in Como.

_____ e) Sandra surprised Paul by kissing him.

Chapter 4

New words 生词

- arrange /ə'reɪndʒ/ *v.* 安排
- arrangement /ə'reɪndʒmənt/ *n.* 安排
- balcony /'bælkəni/ *n.* 阳台
- innocent /'ɪnəsnt/ *a.* 纯洁的
- playfully /'pleɪfəli/ *ad.* 嬉闹地；开玩笑地

Phrases & expressions 短语和表达

- cut off 切断

- make arrangements 作安排
- open up 开启，开始
- pour down (雨) 倾盆而下
- push off 推开
- rather than ... 而不是……
- walk on air 得意扬扬；飘飘然

Cultural note 文化点滴

- Alfa Romeo: 阿尔法 • 罗密欧。意大利著名的轿车和跑车制造公司，创建于 1910 年，总部设在米兰。公司前身最早可追溯至 1907 年。1916 年，出身那不勒斯的尼古拉 • 罗密欧（Nicola Romeo）入主该车厂，并将自己的家族姓氏融入车厂名称中，从而成为今天的阿尔法 • 罗密欧。1986 年，该公司被菲亚特集团（FIAT）收购。

Reading exercise 阅读练习

Match the beginnings and endings.

_____1) Sandra invited Paul to stay

_____2) Paul felt both guilty and excited

_____3) Paul didn't really notice

_____4) Paul didn't think anything

_____5) Paul thought Sandra's parents

a) how expensive Sandra's car was.

b) for a weekend at her family's old house.

c) would also be at the house.

d) about the mysterious locked door.

e) and imagined a new life was beginning.

Chapter 5

New words 生词

- apparently /əˈpærəntli/ *ad.* 显然
- bald /bɔːld/ *a.* 秃顶的；光秃秃的
- border /ˈbɔːdə(r)/ *n.* 边境；边界
- customs /ˈkʌstəmz/ *n.* 海关
- designer /dɪˈzaɪnə(r)/ *a.* 由著名设计师设计的
- ferry /ˈferi/ *n.* 渡船
- melt /melt/ *v.* 融化
- spy /spaɪ/ *n.* 间谍

Cultural notes 文化点滴

- Belaggio: 贝拉焦。典型的意大利小镇，也是科莫湖畔吸引游客最多的一个小镇。Belaggion 的意思是"位于两湖之间"，其独特的地理位置让它拥有异常广阔的视角，据说天气晴好时在后面的山上可以看到米兰的大教堂，甚至可以看到意法边境的欧洲第一高峰勃朗峰。
- Lugano: 卢加诺。瑞士度假胜地提契诺州最大的城镇，不仅是瑞士第三大金融中心和会议、银行业以及商务中心，还是一座公园化的地中海风格的城市，市区别墅与宗教建筑林立。它地处卢加诺湖北部的一座水湾之中，周围环绕着重重青山，景色优美，气候温和宜人。
- Mercedes: 全名"梅赛德斯－奔驰"（Mercedes-Benz），世界著名的德国汽车品牌。1886 年被誉为"汽车的发明者"的卡尔·本茨发明了世界上第一辆三轮汽车；同时，奔驰的另一位创始人戈特利布·戴姆勒发明了世界上第一辆四轮汽车。1926 年 6 月，戴姆勒公司与奔驰公司合并成立了“戴姆勒 – 奔驰”汽车公司。“梅赛德斯”取自奥地利一贵族女儿的名字。

• Villa Carlotta: 卡洛塔别墅。位于科莫的著名景区之一特雷梅佐，建于 1690 年。卡洛塔是一个美丽女子的名字，别墅庄园是她母亲送给她的嫁妆。湖边的白色别墅如今变成了一个小型博物馆，里面收藏了意大利雕塑家安东尼奥·卡诺瓦的作品 Love and Psyche 的复制版（真品在卢浮宫内）。

Reading exercises 阅读练习

1. Who do you think the mystery man in the square was?
2. What do you think was in the package?

Chapter 6

New words 生词

- definitely /ˈdefɪnətli/ *ad.* 绝对地
- drive /draɪv/ *n.* 车道
- embarrassed /ɪmˈbærəst/ *a.* 感到尴尬的
- eventually /ɪˈventʃuəli/ *ad.* 最终
- housekeeper /ˈhaʊskiːpə(r)/ *n.* 管家
- luxury /ˈlʌkʃəri/ *a.* 豪华的；奢侈的
- obviously /ˈɒbviəsli/ *ad.* 显然
- occasion /əˈkeɪʒn/ *n.* 场合；机会

- presumably /prɪˈzjuːməbli/ *ad.* 大概；想必
- probably /ˈprɒbəbli/ *ad.* 很可能
- suspiciously /səˈspɪʃəsli/ *ad.* 怀疑地
- truthfully /ˈtruːθfəli/ *ad.* 真实地
- upset /ʌpˈset/ *a.* 不安的；心烦的
- yacht /jɒt/ *n.* 游艇

Phrases & expressions 短语和表达

- in circles 转圈；兜圈子
- slow down 慢下来，减速
- sports car 跑车
- stare at ... 盯着……

Cultural notes 文化点滴

- Metro: 宝驰。英国最大的汽车制造公司 Austin Rover 于 1979 年制造的一款新型袖珍轿车。
- Portofino: 波托菲诺。位于意大利西北部里格连海岸东面，是著名的旅游海港小镇。在意大利语中，Portofino 意为“边界小港口”。

Reading exercise 阅读练习

Complete the summary.

Sandra invited Paul to stay at the family house in ________. Paul was ________ that her family would be there. Sandra had become very ________ to Paul since Jacky’s death but there were still things he didn’t ________ about her. At the house, Sandra arrived with the man who Paul had seen in ________. His name was ________ and he did some ________ with Sandra's father.

Chapter 7

New words 生词

- antique /æn'tiːk/ *n.* 古董
- blame /bleɪm/ *v.* 责怪
- bodyguard /'bɒdigɑːd/ *n.* 保镖
- connection /kə'nekʃn/ *n.* 关系，联系；人脉
- jewellery /'dʒuːəlri/ *n.* 珠宝
- refill /ˌriː'fɪl/ *v.* 重新加满
- sideboard /'saɪdbɔːd/ *n.* 餐具柜

Phrases & expressions 短语和表达

- close down 关闭；查封；切断
- main course 主菜

Cultural notes 文化点滴

- Giorgio Morandi: 乔治•莫兰迪。以静物画著称，是 20 世纪最受赞誉的意大利画家之一。他既推崇早期文艺复兴大师的作品，也对此后各种流派的大胆探索有着强烈共鸣。
- Murano glass: 穆拉诺玻璃。世界顶尖的玻璃饰品品牌，产于威尼斯附近的穆拉诺岛。一直以来，艺术玻璃加工产业都是威尼斯最重要的经济来源。16 世纪，穆拉诺玻璃制造业达到巅峰。人工吹制出的玻璃更细且纯度高、造型优美，成为欧洲权贵们书桌上不可或缺

的装饰品，更通过在提香和维罗内塞等著名画家的作品中呈现而流芳百世。

Reading exercise 阅读练习

Look at the words in italics. Who is *them*, *she*, *you* etc.?

a) I thanked *them* for inviting me to stay.

b) '*She* has often told us how helpful *you* have been with her business studies.'

c) 'So, what's going on? Shall *we* talk about all this?'

d) '*He* obviously doesn't know about anything.'

e) '*He* didn't realise *you* were a guest of the family.'

Chapter 8

New words 生词

- criminal /ˈkrɪmɪnl/ *n.* 罪犯
- illegal /ɪˈliːgl/ *a.* 非法的
- roll /rəʊl/ *n.* 面包卷

Phrase & expression 短语和表达

- take a deep breath 深呼吸；长叹一口气

Cultural note 文化点滴

- James Bond: 詹姆斯•邦德。《007》系列小说、电影的主角，世界上最著名的秘密特工之一。故事里，他是英国情报机构军情六处的特工，代号007，被授权可以干掉任何妨碍其间谍行动的人。小说原作者是英国作家、前特工伊恩 • 弗莱明（Ian Fleming）。

Reading exercise 阅读练习

Match the beginnings and endings.

____1) Paul saw one of the bodyguards

____2) Paul thought the family business could be

____3) When Sandra suggested visiting England

____4) Paul thought Sandra was being truthful

____5) Sandra was so beautiful that

a) something illegal like selling drugs.

b) when she answered his questions.

c) Paul was doubtful at first.

d) Paul couldn't imagine she was a criminal.

e) doing something near his car.

Chapter 9

New words 生词

- annoyed /əˈnɔɪd/ *a.* 感到生气的
- chew /tʃuː/ *v.* 咬住；咀嚼
- monosyllable /ˈmɒnəsɪləbl/ *n.* 单音节词
- motorway /ˈməʊtəweɪ/ *n.* 高速公路

Phrases & expressions 短语和表达

- be suspicious of ... 怀疑……

- number plate 车号牌
- service station（高速公路）服务站，加油站
- sub-machine gun 冲锋枪，轻型自动枪
- tourist resort 观光胜地

Cultural note 文化点滴

- Clermont-Ferrand: 克莱蒙－费朗。法国中南部城市，是米其林轮胎的诞生地，也是世界著名物理学家帕斯卡的家乡。

Reading exercise 阅读练习

What made Paul suspicious? Put the events in the right order.

_____ a) Sandra received three phone calls but said little.

_____ b) Sandra chewed her lip and looked nervous.

_____ c) Paul thought they were being followed by a yellow Fiat.

_____ d) Paul saw a silver Mercedes like Andrea's.

_____ e) Sandra relaxed after they crossed the border.

Chapter 10

New words 生词

- bang /bæŋ/ *v.* 重击
- croissant /ˈkrwæsɒ̃/ *n.* 羊角面包
- interval /ˈɪntəvl/ *n.* 间隔
- nervousness /ˈnɜːvəsnəs/ *n.* 紧张
- receptionist /rɪˈsepʃənɪst/ *n.* 接待员
- violently /ˈvaɪələntli/ *ad.* 猛烈地；激烈地

Phrases & expressions 短语和表达

- check in 入住；登记；报到
- fed up with ... 受够了……，对……感到厌倦
- on the edge of ... 在……边缘
- take one's time 某人慢慢来，不着急

Cultural notes 文化点滴

• Bourges: 布尔日。法国中部城市，中央大区谢尔省的省会。布尔日靠近法国本土的几何中心，历史上曾是法国重要的宗教文化中心，被著名的《米其林指南》杂志评为最高推荐等级的旅游城市。

• café au lait: 法语意思是加入大量牛奶的咖啡（又叫“欧蕾咖啡”）。在法国，这种花式咖啡是早餐的好伴侣，常用它来搭配羊角面包。它与美式咖啡和意式拿铁最大的区别就是它要求牛奶和浓缩咖啡一同注入杯中。

Reading exercise 阅读练习

True or false?

_____ a) Paul saw the Fiat when they arrived in Issoire.

_____ b) Paul didn't understand what was happening.

_____ c) Sandra was relaxed in the morning.

_____ d) Paul saw the Mercedes leaving the square.

_____ e) Paul knew he had to find out the truth soon.

_____ f) Paul told Sandra that he'd thrown away her phone.

Chapter 11

New words 生词

- authority /ɔːˈθɒrəti/ *n.* 权力；当局；权威
- behave /bɪˈheɪv/ *v.* 表现
- headlight /ˈhedlaɪt/ *n.* 汽车前灯
- horn /hɔːn/ *n.* 鸣笛声
- lane /leɪn/ *n.* 车道；小路
- operation /ˌɒpəˈreɪʃn/ *n.* 行动
- profit /ˈprɒfɪt/ *n.* 利润
- recover /rɪˈkʌvə(r)/ *v.* 恢复
- reproduction /ˌriːprəˈdʌkʃn/ *n.* 复制；复制品
- underneath /ˌʌndəˈniːθ/ *prep.* 在……下面
- unlikely /ʌnˈlaɪkli/ *a.* 不太可能的
- violent /ˈvaɪələnt/ *a.* 猛烈的

Phrases & expressions 短语和表达

- be involved in ... 被卷入……；涉及……
- blow one's nose 某人擤鼻子
- criminal record 犯罪记录
- end up in ... 在……结束；以……为结局
- in one's power 在某人掌控之中
- in the distance 在远处
- on the surface 在表面上
- reach for ... 伸手去够……
- start off 开始做某事；出发
- steering wheel 方向盘

- take a chance 冒险尝试
- windscreen wiper 汽车挡风玻璃雨刷
- works of art 艺术品

Reading exercise 阅读练习

Match the questions and answers.

____1) ‘Sandra, what’s the matter?’

____2) ‘He’s a lot older than you, isn’t he?’

____3) ‘But why didn’t your father report Andrea to the police?’

____4) ‘Why are they following us now?’

____5) ‘What have they put in my car?’

a) ‘I don’t know. Probably paintings that they want to get out of the country.’

b) ‘Leave me alone. You’ve caused nothing but problems all along.’

c) ‘They want to make sure that the operation is successful.’

d) ‘He couldn’t. Don’t you see that my father and his partners were in it too?’

e) ‘Yes, Paul, he is ... but we started a relationship.’

Chapter 12

New words 生词

- disbelief /ˌdɪsbɪˈliːf/ *n.* 不相信，怀疑
- movement /ˈmuːvmənt/ *n.* 行动
- nightmare /ˈnaɪtmeə(r)/ *n.* 噩梦，梦魇
- priceless /ˈpraɪslɪs/ *a.* 价值连城的，无价的

- runaway /ˈrʌnəweɪ/ *a.* 逃离的，逃亡的
- terrorist /ˈterərɪst/ *n.* 恐怖主义者，恐怖分子

Phrases & expressions 短语和表达

- cut in 打断；插嘴；超车
- not least 尤其是；相当重要地
- radio signal 无线电信号
- stretch out 伸出

Cultural notes 文化点滴

• Calvados: 卡尔瓦多斯酒。又称“苹果白兰地”，是法国卡尔瓦多斯省的特产。该酒以苹果为原料，经过发酵、蒸馏，在橡木桶内陈酿而成，呈琥珀色，光泽明亮、发黄，口味微甜。

• Dieppe: 迪耶普。法国北部城市，临拉芒什海峡（英吉利海峡）的港口。原为诺曼底人的一个古老村庄，随着 12 世纪时商业的繁荣，逐渐发展成为城镇。第二次世界大战中遭严重破坏，后来进行了修复，成为法国重要的旅游港口、渔港和商港。

• the Channel: 英吉利海峡。又名“拉芒什海峡”（英语：English Channel，法语：la Manche），是分隔英国与欧洲大陆的法国，并连接大西洋与北海的海峡。最狭窄处又称多佛尔海峡（Strait of Dover），宽仅 34 公里。

Reading exercise 阅读练习

Put the events in the right order.

_____ a) Paul was pleased that Sandra had told him the truth.

_____ b) Early the next morning, they were found by Andrea.

_____ c) Paul realised he really loved Sandra.

_____ d) Paul and Sandra decided to return to Italy.

_____ e) Andrea told them to get ready to leave.

Chapter 13

New words 生词

- corridor /ˈkɒrɪdɔː(r)/ *n.* 走廊，过道
- furnish /ˈfɜːnɪʃ/ *v.* 装饰
- mark /mɑːk/ *n.* 印记
- replace /rɪˈpleɪs/ *v.* 还原
- roughly /ˈrʌfli/ *ad.* 粗略地；粗鲁地
- signal /ˈsɪgnəl/ *v.* 示意
- suburb /ˈsʌbɜːb/ *n.* 郊区

Phrase & expression 短语和表达

- blow sb. a kiss 给某人一个飞吻

Cultural note 文化点滴

- Camembert: 卡蒙贝尔奶酪。被誉为法国十大奶酪之首。这种奶酪较软，质地如同新鲜的蛋糕，容易在高温下融化，适于烹饪，味道清淡，可佐酒或佐餐直接食用。

Reading exercise 阅读练习

Complete the summary.

Paul drove his car to ________ between the Mercedes and the Fiat. They finished their journey at a ________ near the sea. Paul and Sandra were locked up in ________ rooms. Paul couldn't open the ________ of his room. He tried ________ on the wall, and had an answer from Sandra, but she couldn't hear his ________. Paul noticed a door in the ________. He climbed on the table and looked into the ________. He had to get down when he heard the ________ coming.

Chapter 14

New words 生词

- boot /buːt/ *n.* 汽车后备厢
- shoot /ʃuːt/ *v.* 开枪
- swing /swɪŋ/ *v.* 摆，晃
- trainer /ˈtreɪnə(r)/ *n.* 运动鞋
- whisper /ˈwɪspə(r)/ *v.* 低语

Phrases & expressions 短语和表达

- brush down 拍掉灰尘
- check on sb. 检查某人
- get used to ... 适应……
- go off（闹钟）响
- roll over 翻滚；翻身

- switch off 关（电源）
- switch on 开（电源）

Reading exercise 阅读练习

True or false?

____ a) At around one o'clock, Paul heard footsteps coming upstairs.

____ b) The back door was locked.

____ c) Out in the hall Paul turned the light on and listened.

____ d) Paul and Sandra decided to push the car down the road.

____ e) None of the shots hit the car.

Chapter 15

Reading exercise 阅读练习

Match the beginnings and endings.

____ 1) Sandra had saved them some time

____ 2) They drove south through the night,

____ 3) Sandra phoned her father

____ 4) Paul suddenly woke up and realised

____ 5) Sandra wasn't worried because

a) only stopping for food and petrol.

b) Andrea had been delayed.

c) that they had slept too long.

d) by cutting the tyres of both cars.

e) and they arranged to meet at the border.

Chapter 16

New words 生词

- ambulance /ˈæmbjələns/ *n.* 救护车
- brake /breɪk/ *v.* 刹车
- chase /tʃeɪs/ *n.* 追逐
- emergency /iˈmɜːdʒənsi/ *n.* 紧急情况，突发事件
- overtake /ˌəʊvəˈteɪk/ *v.* 超车；赶上
- unconscious /ʌnˈkɒnʃəs/ *a.* 失去知觉的；无意识的
- warning /ˈwɔːnɪŋ/ *n.* 警告

Phrase & expression 短语和表达

- move over 让开

Cultural notes 文化点滴

- Dijon: 第戎。法国东部城市，科多尔省的省会，勃艮第大区首府，是重要的铁路枢纽。该城建于罗马时代，有 13 世纪兴建的大教堂、美术博物馆等著名建筑。
- Lyon: 里昂。法国东南部城市，奥弗涅－罗讷－阿尔卑斯大区的首府和罗讷省的省会。它是法国重要的工业城市和除巴黎之外最重要的科教中心，也是重要的文化与艺术中心。1998 年，里昂老城被联合国教科文组织列为世界文化遗产。

Reading exercise 阅读练习

What does Paul or Sandra say in each situation?

_____ 1) There was the silver Mercedes overtaking a big lorry.

_____ 2) The car obviously didn't like this very much.

_____ 3) Both cars had moved out to follow us ...

_____ 4) I flashed my headlights several times ...

_____ 5) In the far distance I could see a large lorry in the emergency lane.

a) Paul: 'No. This is OK. They're following.'

b) Sandra: 'Careful, Paul. Look ahead!'

c) Sandra: 'And there's Andrea, too! Look!'

d) Sandra: 'I don't think you'd better go any faster.'

e) Sandra: 'And look! There's a police car on the bridge ahead.'

Chapter 17

New words 生词

- divorce /dɪˈvɔːs/ *v.* 离婚
- fax /fæks/ *n.* 传真
- injury /ˈɪndʒəri/ *n.* 伤
- reflection /rɪˈflekʃn/ *n.* 倒影
- robbery /ˈrɒbəri/ *n.* 抢劫，盗窃
- sculpture /ˈskʌlptʃə(r)/ *n.* 雕塑

Phrases & expressions 短语和表达

- crash into ... 撞上……

- remind sb. of ... 提醒某人……

Cultural note 文化点滴

• Interpol: 国际刑警组织 (International Criminal Police Organisation)。成立于 1923 年，最初名为国际刑警委员会，是除联合国之外规模第二大的国际组织，也是全球最大的警察组织，现有 190 多个成员国。1989 年该组织的总部迁到法国里昂。该组织每年召开一次全体大会，日常与各国保持密切关系，组织国际追捕。

Reading exercise 阅读练习

Who ...

____ a) only had a few injuries?

____ b) stayed a long time in hospital?

____ c) died immediately?

____ d) went to prison for ten years?

____ e) was warned to drive carefully?

____ f) was allowed to return to his business?

Paul Sandra Andrea The guard Mr Rovello

Translation
参考译文

意外人生

第 1 章　屋顶瓦片

第5页

屋顶的瓦片掉了。

* * *

在经历了两三百年的雨雪冰霜和风吹日晒之后，屋顶的瓦片掉了。

* * *

在经历了两三百年的雨雪冰霜和风吹日晒之后，屋顶的瓦片从原处掉落到老城的街上。

* * *

在经历了两三百年的雨雪冰霜和风吹日晒之后，屋顶的瓦片从原处掉落到老城的街上，砸到了我妻子头部的正中央。

* * *

在经历了两三百年的雨雪冰霜和风吹日晒之后，屋顶的瓦片从原处掉落到老城的街上，砸到了我妻子头部的正中央，即刻夺走了她的生命。

第 2 章　杰基

第6页

杰基。

关于杰基，我能告诉你们什么呢？

我能告诉你们那个明媚的二月早晨她是什么样子：她踏入清晨的阳光之中，雪从所有的屋顶上落下来，她出去是为了给正在缝制的一条裙子买什么东西。那条裙子是为一顿特殊晚餐准备的——我们结婚三年了。

我的脑海中有一个她的影像库：在办公室；我们一起度过的第一个圣诞节，在苏格兰滑雪；我们的婚礼；我们穿越法国去意大利新家的途中；还有……还有……我还留着给她照过的十张照片，几百张中的十张。

后来，当我能够接受她的离开之后，我浏览了我们在一起时拍的所有照片，并精心挑选了这十张我最喜欢的。然后我把它们放大，放进了一本特制的相册里。在那之后我再也没打开过这本相册。这都是陈年旧事了。我现在老了。

一个充满回忆的老人，脑海里充满了对过去本可能发生的事情的各种臆想。我常常思考，一个非常微小的偶然是如何改变一个人的生活的：如果屋顶的瓦片早一秒或晚一秒落下；如果她去了另一家商店，或走不同的路去那家商店；如果她碰到了个朋友并停下来说话，或者没有碰到朋友停下来说话；她到十字路口时交通信号灯变了……或者……或者……

第7页

这么一个微小的偶然：她当时在那里，那片屋顶的瓦片也在那里。这么一个微小的偶然使得我——时年 27 岁——独自在异国他乡意大利。那么多希望，那么光明的未来，这是一件令人兴奋的事情，一场冒险。去意大利开始新的生活。

我和杰基是在曼彻斯特工作时相识的。我们同时入职。刚开始我们喜欢在一起是因为我们都是新到那儿的，能和一个有着相同处境的人说说话挺好的。工作时聊天逐渐变成酒吧聊天，后来一起出去过周末，到了十一月我们相爱了，计划到苏格兰度过第一个滑雪假日……第一次在一起，第一次和我很爱的人一起出去。

后来事情进展得很快。我们在她 24 岁生日（1 月 20 日）时订了婚，在复活节结了婚。我们在曼彻斯特又工作了两年，在这期间我们觉得想要做些改变。那些年我们去过两次意大利，一次是开车在北部湖区转了转，一次是住在了翁布里亚的一家农舍。

第8页

一到意大利，我们就爱上了那里，因为所有尽人皆知的浪漫的理由——那里的太阳、那里的风景、那里的美食和美酒、那里的人和那里的建筑。什么都很对我们的胃口。我们在曼彻斯特上了意大利语的夜校，学得还不错。

“我的名字叫保罗·莫里斯，你是我的妻子杰基”，我过去常在家里用意大利语这么唱。我们去艺术中心看意大利电影，还常去意大利餐馆吃饭。

我们想改变一下。在曼彻斯特待三年足够了。杰基来自诺里奇，我来自贝德福德，如果不是工作和对方，我们都没什么理由待在曼彻斯特。后来那个特殊的日子到来了。一个周五的晚上，我正在看公司周报“国外”板块的“招聘”栏，这时一条广告从页面跃入我的眼帘：

第9页

科尔沃制药公司
位于科莫的知名公司需要两名充满热情的年轻销售经理，9月1日开始上班。
提供食宿。
提供往返机票。
详情请致电：罗宾逊夫人
0183-7674321

我还记得当时自己拿着报纸跑到厨房喊着“杰基！杰基！科莫！”，兴奋得差点儿把她撞倒。

我们两年前去过科莫，我们俩都喜欢那座城市和那里的湖。而现在，有了在这么美好的地方工作的机会！

杰基不一会儿就变得比我还要兴奋，她立马给罗宾逊夫人打了电话。那天晚上我们无法入眠，聊着如果得到那份工作会出现的所有奇妙的可能。接下来的周一，我们收到了申请表和详细的工作介绍。一切似乎都很完美。这家公司相当不错，他们提供位于老城中心的一套公寓。长话短说，我们申请了工作，进行了面试，在五月底获得了工作机会，我们接受了。

第10页

意大利。我们要去那里生活了。离开湿冷的曼彻斯特，投入火热的夏日、碧蓝的湖水、飘雪的冬天、迷人的景色、滑雪……这一切都将永远属于我们！

我们离开了现在的工作。所有人，我们的朋友、家人，甚至是公司的同事，都认为我们为了国外不可预知的生活离开英国稳定的工作是不明智的。我们料到了他们会那么说。我们并不介意。我们把自己的东西打了包，留下一些给了双方父母，其他的用火车托运到了意大利。八月中旬，我们度了两周的假，然后开车穿过法国前往科莫。

我们于八月底到达，以便在九月份开始工作前把公寓收拾好。从我们在曼彻斯特相遇以来已经过去三年了。如此短的时间里发生了那么多变化！

即使现在，这么多年后，我仍然清晰地记得当时在科莫的感觉是多么美好。杰基和意大利——我过去常对自己说——是我生命中的两个挚爱，而我同时拥有了二者！我是多么幸运的人啊！

我知道杰基也是这么觉得的。我们对彼此的爱与日俱增。所有事情我们都一起做，一起工作，一起玩乐。我们比以往任何时候都要亲密。我们十分喜欢我们的工作。与我们一起共事的意大利人都很友好，我们很容易就交到了朋友。在家里，所有的邻居都很热情，乐于助人。一切看起来都很完美。

第11页

然而，五个月之后，她却不在了。我再也看不到她那双灰色的眼睛深情地望着我了；再也看不到她枕头上的头发了，就像莱纳德·科恩那首歌里唱的——“(枕头上) 熟睡的金色风暴”。什么都没有了，只剩下孤零零的我。

第 3 章　桑德拉

第12页

当你的生活中突然出现一个大坑时你怎么办？你要么掉进去，要么开始把它填满。

杰基被葬在了位于英国的故乡。对于我，这一切就像是一场噩梦。之后发生的一切也像是一场梦。

我要填写许多文件，要见许多人，要回英国许多次。但在我的脑海里有一件事是清楚的：我想要留在科莫。杰基也会想要我留下的。那是一个我不想放弃的美梦。我的家人和杰基的家人都认为我应该回英国，和熟悉的人、关心我的人在一起。我知道那不对。那样的话仿佛我是在逃避。我得回去，用自己的方式面对。

于是，杰基下葬两周后，我直接回到了科莫上班。我努力工作，经常整天忙碌，在办公室待到很晚。有时候我晚上还把工作带回家去做。我甚至接管了杰基的一些工作来帮公司，也帮自己填满空闲的时间。

第13页

每到周末我就开车去山里什么地方，滑一天的雪，直到累得筋疲力尽。人们很善良。我收到了很多同事的邀请，但我没怎么接受。我一个人去短期度假，这些假期都是我和杰基之前就计划好的……

我觉得我和桑德拉的友情始于二月份。桑德拉曾在杰基的团队工作。她和杰基看起来不太一样，但是……也许我只是孤独罢了。我和她的熟悉程度也就是在办公室说一声“你好”，圣诞假期前和他们团队一起吃过一次比萨饼。有一两次我发现自己在盯着她看。有一次她看到了我在看她，便回敬了我一个微笑。

但我想一个人留在对杰基的回忆中。一月份的一个晚上，我在下班往家走的路上碰到了桑德拉。我们在冬日的街道上边走边聊。十分钟后我们道别时——在寒冷的夜晚里温暖地握了握手——我意识到自己的心跳比平时快了，脸有些发烫。我感觉自己就像是个第一次约会的男孩儿。

后来我又完全忘记了桑德拉。二月份我接管了杰基的营销团队。第一次开会，我走进房间时，看到了桑德拉，她就坐在我对面。我一开始差点儿说不出话来。

第14页

桑德拉在会议期间帮了我不少忙——她是那种所有经理刚到一个团队时都需要的人。会议结束时别人都走了，她留了下来。她朝我走过来。

"保罗，"她说，"我想告诉你我对杰基的事情感到非常难过。"接着她做了件令人惊讶的事。她轻轻地亲了一下我的脸，然后走了，给我留下了她的香水味儿和她柔软的双唇接触过我皮肤的感觉。我感到很困惑。

那晚回到家，我在杰基死后第一次哭了。我哭了好几个小时，想着我和她在一起的全部生活，所有美好的时光，以及我知道自己在努力掩饰的空虚。在这之前和之后我都没有哭得这么厉害。为她而哭，为我们而哭，为我们的梦想而哭，为我……然后我意识到，我不能再装作像杰基还活着那样继续生活、工作和度假了。第二天早上走进浴室时，我看着自己红肿的眼睛和苍白的脸，我想这应该是杰基去世后我新生活的开始。

正是桑德拉帮我下定了这个决心。是的，最终，我可以说桑德拉帮了我。且不说我和桑德拉之间发生的所有事，她那时确实帮了我的忙。会议后的那个吻改变了我内心的某些东西，而改变正是我在失去杰基后所需要的。

第16页

第二次会议后我和桑德拉聊了一会儿，我们聊着天穿过小城走了一段路。那成了我期待的事情。我特别用心地准备着那些团队会议，我的新团队工作很卖力。我知道每个下午的会议之后，我都可以和桑德拉一起走上几分钟。

复活节时我去逛了逛威尼托的别墅区，原本我是计划和杰基一起去的，我一个人去了。我常想起杰基来，想到她会多么喜欢这次旅行，但我也会想起桑德拉。我从威尼托给桑德拉寄了张明信片。我只是因为想知道她在科莫住在哪里，于是得到了她的住址。但独自身处在那些廉价旅馆的黑暗中，在看了一天绝妙的建筑后，我发现自己常常想起她来。我想象着她在办公室的画面——丰满的唇上挂着的微笑、深棕色的眼睛和深棕色的齐肩秀发。我在脑海中一遍遍地像放电影般回放她那个轻轻的吻。我发觉自己开始好奇和她真正地亲吻、拥抱会是什么感觉。

不得不承认，我对这些想法感到愧疚。毕竟杰基去世才四个月。

但我忍不住想桑德拉。于是我给她寄了张明信片，并签了名：“爱你的，保罗。”

第 4 章　一个乡村周末

第17页

四月末，我们又开了一次团队会议，之后像往常一样在城里散步时，她突然问："保罗，你下周末有安排吗？"

"没什么特别的事，"我回答，"怎么了？"

"你愿意去马格雷廖我家的老房子吗？老房子在山上。离开科莫出去转转对你有好处。"

我立刻回答了她："我愿意。"听到自己回答得那么爽快，我很吃惊。但令我更吃惊的是，她用双手捧住我的脸颊，吻了我的嘴。起初，我并没有回吻她，但后来我用双臂搂住她的腰，这个吻变成了一个漫长而深情的吻。感觉真好，就像我一直在等待的某样东西。如此温暖、充实，如此令人兴奋，就如同吃了一种新奇的水果一样。

然后我第一次一路把她送回家，路上又停下来亲吻了好几次，并计划周末的行程。

第18页

回到公寓的时候，我感觉自己轻飘飘的，仿佛走在云端。愧疚与兴奋交织在一起——就如同是我瞒着妻子有了外遇一样。我无法入睡。那是个美丽的夜晚，于是我从冰箱里拿出一瓶白葡萄酒，坐在阳台上。我喝着酒，看着月亮从山上升起……新的生活开始了。

周六早上九点，桑德拉按照约定开车到达时正下着大雨。我已经准备好了，从公寓门口跑出去上了她的车，我们亲吻了许久。我太兴奋了，几乎没注意到那是辆价格不菲的阿尔法·罗密欧——靠她在科尔沃制药公司的工资根本买不起这辆车。

我们沿着湖边大道开着车时，车内仿佛有一种电流在我们之间涌动，大雨遮住了湖面和群山。这使得车内的世界更加神秘，更加与世隔绝。我问她我们要去的房子的事——我们之前做准备时她没有多说什么，只是说晚上会冷，要带暖和的衣服和步行靴。她说，那里本来是属于她的曾祖父母的。她父母刚结婚时在那里住过，但现在那里只是一个周末逃离喧嚣的地方。

第19页

最近几年她和她哥哥不怎么去那儿了。他们想去旅行，看看其他的地方。世界上并不是只有科莫和马格雷廖。她笑了起来。我喜欢她的笑声，自然而然、无拘无束。一小时后我们到了，把车停在树下，在雨中经过菜园，沿着湿润的小径向房子走去。房子里面很黑。

“你父母呢？”我问。

“在科莫，”她回答，“怎么了？”

“哦，我以为他们会在这儿，周末种种菜什么的。”我惊讶地答道。她之前说是家里的老房子，我以为她的家人会在那儿。

她缓慢地转过身，走过来站在我面前，她的眼睛在昏暗的光线中几乎是黑色的，但依然闪着光彩。她说：“如果他们在这儿的话，我干吗要带你来？”

我好像说了些“哦，这样啊”之类的傻话，想用胳膊搂住她。她顽皮地把我推开了。

“过一会儿吧，”她说，“我们先把这里搞暖和。”

接下来的一小时里，她忙着把所有房间的取暖器打开，而我在客厅用木头生火。接着我们把带来的吃的放进冰箱，她煮了咖啡。火渐渐旺起来，我们坐在沙发上喝咖啡。十一点半了。

第20页

“我带你到处看看吧。”她说罢带着我在房子里转起来。楼下有间大客厅、一个厨房兼餐厅和一间现代化的浴室，楼上有三间小卧室。

“这是我小时候住的卧室，”她在楼上最小的卧室里说，“夏天每天早晨我常躺在这里，看着太阳从那座山上升起来……瞧，太阳要出来了！我带你看看院子吧。”

我们穿上了靴子，因为外面的地面依然很湿。我们手牵手走着，她带我看她祖父母以前养鸡的地方、她父母今年种的蔬菜，还有她小时候常在那儿玩的苹果树。

“那下面是什么？”我指着通向房子一侧一扇棕色门的石阶问。

“哦，现在什么也不是，”她说，“以前他们常在那儿存放酒和蔬菜。”

我正要转身离开，这时看到了门上的锁——那是一把新锁。

第21页

“可是桑德拉……”我开口说，但她已朝着房子往回走了，说着午餐要吃什么。她把几种意大利人总是很快可以做好的、美味而简单的饭菜混到一起，我们就着我带来的上等红酒吃起来……酒本来是我带给她父母的！在我往快熄灭的火上添木头时，她不见了。我向窗外望去。外面又下起了倾盆大雨。我本希望午餐后我们能一起到村子里散散步，但我可不想在雨里走路。

“又下雨了，桑德拉，”我喊道，“今天下午我们要干什么？”

没有回答。我走进厨房——她不在。我觉得她可能去洗手间了，于是走回到暖和的客厅里。

“保罗，”我听到，“保罗，你能上来一下吗？”我爬上楼梯，想着出了什么问题。最大的那间卧室的门开着，我于是走了进去。“你想干什么……？”桑德拉躺在床上，微笑着。

“我觉得这里可能是个度过下雨的周六下午的好地方。”她说。

“嗯，看起来比雨中的村子更有意思。”我费了好大劲才说。

现在回想起来，那可能是我有生以来度过的最愉快的周末。那之后我有过几段感情经历。那个周末我们没有逛马格雷廖，也没怎么看房子的其他地方，只是去了几趟厨房拿吃的和酒！

第22页

周日晚上回到科莫的公寓时，我感到身体极度疲倦，但有一种全新的愉悦感。我并不是想拿杰基作比较，但和桑德拉在一起就像是一场新的成人冒险，而不是之前我熟知的和杰基在一起时的那种更加纯真的爱。

第 5 章　瑞士之谜

第23页

“今天下午我们去卢加诺吧。”桑德拉突然说。那是六月末的一个周六，我们刚吃完午饭。自马格雷廖之旅后我们在一起度过了几个周末和许多夜晚，大多数时候是在我的公寓里。在科莫她还是和父母住在一起。

“什么？”我吃惊地问。通常，在下午，我们会开车去贝拉焦镇吃蛋糕，或去卡洛塔别墅的花园散步。“我们干吗要去瑞士？”

“换一换呗。”她回答，“你去过吗？那儿不远，你知道的。”

“我知道。我和杰基去年十一月份去过。”那时我已经可以谈论杰基了，仿佛我们的婚姻在几年前而不是几个月以前结束的。桑德拉改变了一切。

“而且我们还可以开你的车。”她说。

“好的。”我同意了，很高兴有开车的机会——通常都是她开车载我们去这儿去那儿，她说她更认识路。而且她的那辆阿尔法·罗密欧也更舒适些。

第24页

“我们开你的车吧。”我说。

“车暂时不能用了。”她说。我当时并没有想到她要用我的车去瑞士是有原因的，直到后来我才明白。

“不过先送我回家吧，”她接着说，“我得拿点儿东西。”

开车到贝拉焦后，我们坐渡轮过了科莫湖到达梅纳焦，然后翻山越岭来到了卢加诺湖。之后我们沿着湖边一路去了海关。在那里意大利官员直接让我们过了边境，但瑞士官员检查了我们的护照，并询问我们要去哪里。接着我们继续前往卢加诺，并停好了车。

我们亲吻后走向广场上一个极其整洁的咖啡厅，点了两大碗瑞士人特别喜欢的水果奶油冰激凌。

片刻后，桑德拉环顾广场四周，看了看手表，然后站了起来。“我去下洗手间。”她说完就消失在了咖啡厅里。冰激凌到了，我开始吃自己的那份，琢磨着为什么桑德拉去了那么久。五分钟后我站起来想看看她在哪里。我在咖啡厅里没看到她。出于某种原因，我从花盆上方往我们座位后的广场望去……桑德拉就在那儿，大约一百米开外。

第25页

她正表情严肃地和一个穿着讲究的光头男人说话，他戴着名牌墨镜，站在一辆银色奔驰车的旁边。那个人显然很生气。我看见桑德拉打开包给了他一个小包裹。接着她说了些别的，然后转身朝我们的咖啡厅走回来。

我又坐了下来，吃了点儿冰激凌。我的心跳得很快，想知道发生了什么。这次来卢加诺的意外旅行、开我的车、见那个有钱人、包裹……简直就像是间谍片里的情景！我不知该不该问桑德拉此事。

“抱歉，保罗。”她回到桌边说，亲了亲我的脸。“要排队，后来我又花了很长时间化妆。”

“吃冰激凌吧，要化了。”我听到自己说。显然我决定先保持冷静，晚些时候再尽力查出是怎么回事。

第6章　夏日假期

第27页

在意大利的夏天里，一切仿佛慢了下来。大多数人到海边或山里去度假。我没怎么思考假期做什么。我和杰基曾经聊过开车去意大利南部转转，尽管我仍然心向往之，但我不想一个人去。

卢加诺之旅大约一星期后，桑德拉提起了假期的话题。我们当时躺在我科莫公寓的床上，她转过身表情严肃地问：“暑期你准备做什么，保罗？”

“我还没怎么想过。”我诚实地说，“你准备做什么？”

“嗯，我通常前两周在我们海边的家里度过，在波多菲诺。你去过那里吗？”

“没有，”我回答，“不过我看过一些照片。那里很美。”

第28页

“你想去吗？”她问。

“嗯……呃……想。那很好啊。但是……嗯……我住在哪里呢？”

“哦，地方多的是，”她回答，“我们会给你找张床的。”

“我们？”我问。

“哦，对。这一次我家所有人都会在，”她说，接着补充说，“不会像在马格雷廖那样！”

“哦，这样啊。”我回答道，感到有点儿失望。但我同意了。我当然要同意。为什么要拒绝呢？她很美丽，而我在一个美丽的国家里。如果我知道之后会发生什么，我就会拒绝了。肯定的。

桑德拉比我提前几天出发去了波多菲诺。我决定在开车从科莫去波多菲诺的路上参观几个地方。我参观了托斯卡纳区的佛罗伦萨、卢卡和比萨，之后沿着海岸往北一直开到了波多菲诺。狭窄的道路上挤满了夏天度假的车辆，但风景很美——绿树覆盖的山脉一直延伸到地中海蔚蓝的水域中。

那个地方曾经是个渔村，海边是一群红黄相间的房屋，另一侧是一座城堡。水面上满是船只，其中很多是豪华游艇。在夏天午后强烈的阳光照耀下，这里棒极了。

第29页

我迫不及待地想见到桑德拉。我已经有一周多没见到她了，我发现自己竟如此想念她，我很吃惊。我意识到自从杰基去世后，她已经变得对我十分重要了。

可是我还是不了解她。在马格雷廖的那个锁着的房间，她开的昂贵的车，去卢加诺的旅行，神秘的见面和包裹，以及她从未和我聊过工作以外的生活。(她曾经说过他们做“进出口”的“家族生意”，她有时候会去帮忙。)

在这次开车穿越意大利的旅途中，我才真正思考起另一件事：有那么两三次她为什么不能见我？她说过什么“要去别的地方”，但什么也没解释。不过我也没问太多问题，不是地点不合适就是时间不合适。而且我觉得如果我问得太多——比如关于卢加诺的包裹——她会断绝我们的关系，我又会孑然一身了。而我当时不确定我是否想再次孤身一人。我还希望到达波多菲诺时，能找到这些问题的一些答案……

第30页

我终于找对了路。几乎就在山顶，维亚·卡多纳路 19 号——贝拉维斯塔别墅。从那里能俯瞰大海和城堡，景色迷人。我想象她的家人在这样一座高大的建筑里有一套公寓，这座建筑很可能曾是某个富商的度假之处。桑德拉耀眼的阿尔法·罗密欧、几辆奔驰和一辆亮黄色的菲亚特跑车停在了一个大花园旁的停车场。真是个奢华的地方！

我把自己又脏又旧的英国宝驰车停在桑德拉的车旁边，下了车。在门口我找不到任何姓氏显示哪幢公寓是哪家的，于是我按下了我能找到的唯一一个门铃。开门的是一位衣着像管家的中年妇女。

“找谁？”她冷冷地问，上下打量着我。

“桑德拉·罗韦洛住这儿吗？”我问。

“亚历桑德拉小姐出去了。你是谁？”她回答。

“哦，我叫保罗。保罗·莫里斯，桑德拉是……”我不必找到合适的措辞，因为这时一辆驶入车道的汽车发出的声音让我们都转过身去。当我意识到那是桑德拉的时候，我瞠目结舌。她正和那个在卢加诺见过面的男人坐在那辆银色的奔驰车里。

第31页

桑德拉看了看我那辆脏兮兮的车，接着朝着我和管家站着的地方望过来，她的表情非常严肃。她下车的时候我朝她走过去。

“哦，保罗，”她勉强笑着说，“你到了真好。瞧，安德里亚——这位是保罗·莫里斯，我在科尔沃的新经理。保罗，这位是安德里亚·卡尔塔。”

这是个让人为难的情形。我努力保持礼貌，但和他握手时感到很尴尬。安德里亚毫无兴致地看了看我。

“我进去了，亚历桑德拉，”他说，“待会儿见。再见，莫里斯先生。很高兴见到你。”

我站在可爱的花园里，后面是奢华的别墅，旁边站着一位漂亮的意大利女士，我的大脑一片空白，不知道该说些什么，或者做些什么。我盯着地面。

“保罗，”安德里亚进去后桑德拉说道，“我们在花园里走走吧。”我什么也说不出来。她过来拉住我的手。

“来告诉我你的假期是怎么过的，”她说，“你去了些什么地方？”

我并不想去，但还是和她走进了后花园，坐在一个满是鱼的水池旁边的长椅上。我感觉自己就像是池子里的一条鱼，一圈一圈地转着，不知道自己身在何处。

第32页

“保罗，”她说着想拉住我的手，“你怎么这么不高兴？”

“嗯，我应该有其他什么感受吗？你邀请我来这儿，然后你……你……你和另外一个男的开车进来。”我回答。

“可我们之间没什么，保罗，”她说，“他只是我们家的一个朋友，仅此而已。”我转身望着她的眼睛。

“桑德拉，我在卢加诺看到你见他了。”我直言。

“哦，他在……呃……”她开始说。

“算了吧，桑德拉。”我轻声说，准备站起来。她把我拉回到长椅上。

“我爸爸想要我给他带点儿东西，”她说，“他们有时候做生意，保罗。是真的！没别的了。”

“真的？”我怀疑地问。

“真的。”她回答。然后她吻了我。我现在意识到她当时吻我可能只是想让我住嘴，那样她就不需要再解释什么了。但当时我觉得我可能对一切——我的生活——都感到莫名其妙，于是我回吻了她，持久而深情。

第33页

“对不起，保罗。”她又说。

“嗯，我看我还是走吧。你父亲的朋友显然不想让我在这里。”

“不，你别走。你既然已经来了就一定要留下。别管他，他就那样儿。来吧，”她说着牵起我的手，“我们去拿你的东西，给你找个房间。”

第 7 章　陷得更深

第34页

那天晚上八点半，我从房间下来和桑德拉的父母喝餐前酒。安德里亚和另外两个男的被介绍为与她父亲合作时间比较长的生意伙伴。还有两个身材高大的男人，看起来像是保镖，但被介绍为家族生意的员工。大家都很客气，我感谢他们邀请我住在那儿。

“哦，别客气，”罗韦洛太太说，她身上戴满了金首饰，“我们很高兴你能来看我们。桑德拉一直在说你的好话，她常跟我们说你对她的商务学习帮助很大。”

我微笑着感谢了她，接着看向桑德拉。商务学习！她到底跟他们说了些什么？她看起来很天真、很冷静，冲着我微笑，然后给我倒满酒。晚餐吃了很久，饭菜很可口，主菜是当地的鱼。饭后罗韦洛先生说他还有事要谈，把别的男士带到了另一个房间，关门时说：“请随意喝点儿酒，看看电视。”

第35页

桑德拉的母亲也消失了，留下我和桑德拉。我从餐具柜上拿了一瓶威士忌给自己倒了一大杯，喝了一大口说：“到底怎么回事？我们要不要谈谈这一切？”

桑德拉过来浅浅地亲了亲我的脸。我坐了下来。我什么都稀里糊涂的。我环顾着房间：昂贵的古董家具，墙上有一幅乔治·莫兰迪的画，穆拉诺玻璃饰品……罗韦洛家真是相当有钱啊。

“明天早上再说吧。”她说。她牵着我的手，把我带到楼上我的卧室。在门口她说：“恐怕得分房睡。我累了。晚安。”接着她迅速亲了我一下就走了。

我在房间里坐下，喝着威士忌。房间里有台电视机，我打开浏览各个频道，都是周六晚上通常播放的节目——游戏节目和老电影，我都不感兴趣。我一直在想着另一个房间里的桑德拉，想着她脱掉衣服钻到被子里，还有我有多想和她在一起。

我知道自己无法马上入睡，于是决定去呼吸呼吸新鲜空气。我蹑手蹑脚地走下楼，从侧门出去，留着门以便我还能回来。

第36页

花园里还有太阳的余温，闻起来花香四溢。那是个美丽的夜晚。我绕着房子散步，忽然发现自己来到了一间开着窗的房间底下。我能听到里面有人说话。

“……那就是她为什么邀请他来这儿……”安德里亚说。

“是，但是这种情况下非常危险。”罗韦洛先生说。

“哦，不会。我不觉得，”安德里亚说，“他显然什么都不知道。你瞧卢加诺那次多轻松。那是个非常聪明的点子。”

“得了吧，我们只不过是走运罢了。”罗韦洛先生争辩道。

“但你认为桑德拉能说服他去英国吗？”其中一个生意伙伴说。

“我觉得他会做她要求的任何事。”安德里亚回答。

我无法相信自己听到的话，努力去捕捉每个字。

“很好，因为如果我们能把东西尽快弄到伦敦去的话，鉴于安德里亚和美国那边的关系被切断了，这样也许能帮我们继续在那边的市场上立足……”其中一位伙伴说。

第37页

“但不能让他知道任何事，”安德里亚说，“亚历桑德拉需要……”

那是我听到他们对话的最后一句，但直到一个小时左右之后我在房间醒来才知道。我躺在床上，桑德拉坐在我身边。我头上有条湿毛巾，头疼得厉害。

“你还得休息一会儿，”她说，“傻小子！”

我眼睛看得不是很清楚。“发生什么事了？”我问。

“哦，可怜的保罗。你夜里在房子外面干什么？有个保镖以为你是贼，他没认出你是家里的客人。”

“嗯，那也没必要打我啊。”我说着轻轻地摸着头。

“我知道。对不起。恐怕保镖们都没那么温柔。不过现在，保罗，你得睡一会儿。”桑德拉说着把毛巾放下，擦干手。

“可是桑德拉……”我开口说。

第38页

“现在先别说，保罗，”她回答，“睡吧，我们早上再说。”

她亲了亲我的头顶，离开了，丢下我一个人在黑暗的房间里忍受着头痛，以及比几小时前刚到贝拉维斯塔别墅时更多的疑问。

我躺在那里，脑海里回想着发生的所有事情。我非常害怕，感觉自己像一只被擒获的动物。这些人想要从我这儿得到什么？我是否应该现在起身离开？我如何能摆脱这可怕的境地？可恶的桑德拉！可恶的杰基！可恶的屋顶瓦片！我的怒气把我带回到现实中。我不能责怪自己去世的妻子。这是我的错。我那么喜欢桑德拉，杰基去世后我那么需要她，以至于什么都没想清楚。最后，我睡着了。

第 8 章　准备

第39页

我早早地醒来了。大约是四点。我需要透透气，于是去了房间外面的阳台。天还黑着，但我能听到海水的声音。我望着对面的城堡，上面有灯光在闪烁。风吹拂着树林，美不胜收。站在那儿时，我听到下面有声音。我低头望去，正好看见其中一个保镖站在我的汽车旁边。不过，停车场还很黑，我没看清楚他到底在干什么，但那让我非常不高兴。

从我听到那些“美国那边的关系”和“把东西弄到伦敦去”的话之后，我觉得我终于弄明白了他们的“家族生意”是什么了：贩毒或是别的非法买卖。当我把晚上听到的和之前看到的——马格雷廖锁住的门和卢加诺的包裹——联系到一起后，现在一切都变得非常清晰了。为什么我之前没想到呢？为什么我在卢加诺时没说点儿什么呢？我觉得自己好愚蠢，让自己陷入这样的麻烦里。现在我也明白了些别的事。

第40页

看起来桑德拉一直以来都在利用我。她已经利用过我一次，把什么东西——可能是毒品，或是金子——带到了卢加诺，而且是放在我的车里。试想一下，我们要是被抓住了会如何！她邀请我来这里只是因为她想说服我和她带点儿别的东西去英国——这次的东西更重要。我以前真是愚蠢！

我回到房间，躺下后回想着所见所闻的所有奇怪的事，最后又睡着了。十点左右，我被桑德拉叫醒，她带来了咖啡和面包卷。

“你好，”她边高兴地说着边拉开了窗帘，“今天早上感觉怎么样了？”

“还行，我感觉。”我回答着，轻轻地摸了摸头。

“嗯，这是给你准备的美味早餐，”她微笑着说，“吃好了来池边的花园找我吧。我有话跟你说。”

“桑德拉……”我开口说，但她已经走了。于是我吃了早饭，洗漱穿戴好，下楼步入弥散着热气的地中海花园去找桑德拉。她看见我走近，站起来向我走过来。

第41页

“你好，保罗，”她拉住我的手说，“你看起来好多了。关于昨晚的事我很抱歉。”

“是吗？”我怀疑地说。我们又坐在了池边的椅子上，她亲了亲我的脸。在发生了所有这些事后，我不确定该怎么做、该说什么了。

“当然啦，”她说，“你现在感觉如何？”

“还行。”我说。她又亲了亲我。

“那就好，因为我刚想到了一个好主意。回科莫上班前我们还有很多时间，我们去趟英国怎么样？”

“我们为什么要去？”我简单地问。我想知道在我昨晚听到了那些话之后她会怎么回答，我还想知道她到底对“家族生意”了解多少。

“你可以带我到处看看。我们可以在英国一起度个小假。你觉得呢？”

我思考了很久才说话。

“我想和你去英国，桑德拉，非常想。我喜欢和你在一起，你真的是我唯一的朋友。但出发前，我需要你回答一两个问题。”

“什么问题，保罗？”她问。

第42页

“我需要知道安德里亚和在卢加诺发生的事，还有我昨晚听到的事，”我说，“我需要一些诚实的回答。”

“我跟你说过安德里亚了，”桑德拉说，“他只是我父亲的一个生意伙伴。他管理我们出口美国的事务，但是最近那里出了些问题。所以这周末他来这儿和我父亲一起商量怎么办。”

“那我们那次为什么要去卢加诺？”我问。

“就是下午出去逛逛，”她说，“也是因为我父亲要我去见安德里亚，把他落下的东西给他。”

“什么东西？”我死死地盯着她问。她也盯着我。

“我不知道，保罗，”她回答，“文件，或者别的什么东西。我在科尔沃制药公司工作，而不是在我父亲的公司。那些跟我无关。我只是帮我父亲办点儿事。”

她看起来像是说了实话。也许这一切只是我的想象，也许我只是年轻时看过太多詹姆斯·邦德的电影了！

或者也许我只是情愿相信她。我看着她。她非常漂亮。我发现很难把她视为一名罪犯。也许他们昨晚只是在谈正常的生意，可是为什么那个保镖要打我呢？

第43页

“好，但为什么昨晚那个保镖打我呢？”我问。

“我跟你说过了，”桑德拉回答，“他以为你是盗贼。他们非常警惕。你看起来可疑。不管怎样，你那可怜的头现在怎么样了？”

她伸出手，将我的头扭过去看被打的地方。接着她把我的脸转向她，吻了我一下。

“看起来好多了，”她说，“那我们到底去不去英国？”

我深深地叹了口气。

“好吧。”我说。

“好。我们明天就出发，”她说，“我想尽快离开这儿！”

第9章　进入法国

第44页

第二天上午十点，我们已经开车行驶在热那亚西边的高速公路上，离法国边境不远了。海面折射的阳光照到周边环绕的山上。到目前为止，旅途还比较顺利。然而，当我们到达边境时，我们碰到了没有料想到的缓慢行驶的车流。我们开近海关时，到处都是穿着特警服、手持冲锋枪的警察。

我的心怦怦直跳。也许我终究还是卷入了非法的勾当！也许我就要被抓起来，最后被关进大牢！我看了看桑德拉。她咬着嘴唇，看起来很紧张。

但警察只是招了招手示意我们通过。显然他们正在找的是别人。当车辆在法国一侧的边境开始加速时，桑德拉看起来轻松多了。我又开始生了疑心。如果只是和男友度假，她的行为就显得不太正常了。也许我们真的在车里装了什么东西。

第45页

“桑德拉，”我说，“你确定我们没有做什么违法的事吗？”

“为什么这么问？”她问，“你这话是什么意思？”

“嗯，只是刚才在边境那边有警察的时候你看起来那么紧张……”

“哦，求你了，保罗！”她说，“你所有的问题我都听够了。别这么疑神疑鬼的。”她现在对我没有那么温柔了。

之后我们很长一段时间都没说话。我们行驶在著名的旅游景点戛纳和尼斯附近时，以及穿过红色的普罗旺斯乡村时，路上车辆非常多。到三点钟时，我感到又饿又累，还需要上厕所。“我们该在哪里停车？”我问。

“我们在下一个服务站停吧，”她说，“我也需要下车。”在服务站，我先给车加了油，接着把车停在了商店前。我去了厕所。我正洗着手时，一个清洁工从另一扇门进来，愉快地用法语说了声“您好，先生”。

出于某种原因，我从那扇打开的门向外望去。那是在楼的后侧。我正看着，一辆银色的奔驰车从停车场开到了路上。我确定那是安德里亚的车，尽管我没有看到车牌和开车的人。

第46页

我走进商店。透过大窗户，我可以看见桑德拉站在我们的车旁边。她正通过手机和别人用意大利语快速通话。我买了些橙汁和矿泉水，出来朝我的车走去。桑德拉正在车边等着。

“你刚才在和谁通话？”我问。

她看起来有点儿恼怒。难道她不愿意我知道她刚刚在和别人通话？

“你怎么了，保罗？”她问，“你对所有事、所有人都怀疑。我刚才就是和我父亲通话，告诉他我一切都好。他担心我。”

“知道了。”我说。但现在我真不怎么相信她了；我现在无法相信她了，在我认为我看到了安德里亚的奔驰车后。

我们整个下午都在开车。她生我的气，但即使那样都让我心生怀疑：如果她没有什么要隐藏的，为什么要生气？她把地图册摊开在膝盖上。我们唯一的交流内容是关于方向和道路的。桑德拉的手机响了三次，她每次都用一个意大利语字回答——“是”“不”和“好”，这让我什么也听不出来。

第47页

我一直目视前方，通过后视镜观察安德里亚的银色轿车是否在，但它没有出现。但一段时间之后，我的确觉得我们被远远地跟踪了。我常注意到我们后面隔着几辆车的位置有一辆黄色的菲亚特跑车。那辆车能比我的小宝驰跑得快得多，但我不理解它为何只在我们后面跟着。这时我想起来，我到波多菲诺的别墅时，停车场也有一辆和那辆车一模一样的黄色菲亚特。

我们一直行驶在法国火辣的夏日阳光中。红色的南方大地变成了岩石，接着变成了更浓绿的丘陵。随着夜幕降临，我们越来越靠近克莱蒙-费朗了。

“我累了。”我的话打破了长久以来的沉默，这段时间里我只能自己思来想去，“也饿了。”

“好的，”桑德拉说，“我们找个地方过夜吧。”

第 10 章　不愉快的行驶

第48页

半小时后，我把车停在了伊索瓦村的邮政旅社门前。我下车后环顾四周，没有看到银色的奔驰和黄色的菲亚特。但那并不意味着什么。旅馆里，桑德拉用流利的法语在前台办理入住，我们上三楼到了我们的房间。

“我出去一小会儿。”桑德拉说。她马上离开了。我在床上躺下，累得没有问她为什么和去哪里。半小时后她又出现了。“好了，”她高兴地说，“该吃晚饭了。我在广场对面找了家不错的小餐馆，我给咱俩预订了半小时后的座位。你还饿吗？”

“我能吃下一匹马！”我说着站起来。我朝她走过去，用胳膊搂住她。

“咱们和好吧，桑德拉。我讨厌咱俩这么长时间不说话。”

第49页

“我想跟你友好相处，”她说，“但你总是不停地说那些关于我的难听的话……”

“对不起，”我说，“但你要知道，理解发生的这些事情对于我来说有多难。”

“真没什么要理解的，保罗，”她简单地回答，“享受我们的假期就好了。”

我们亲吻着，漫长而深情的吻。那是我们那天第一个吻，感觉很棒。我难以自禁。

在餐馆吃完了一顿美味的晚餐后，我好好地冲了个澡，一头倒在了床上。开了一天车，我非常疲倦，头一挨着枕头就睡着了。我有感觉，在我睡着时桑德拉离开了房间，后来又回来了，但我不知道她做了什么。

* * *

第二天早上六点半，桑德拉已经完全穿戴好，并化好了妆。她叫醒我。

“那边桌上有加牛奶的咖啡和羊角面包，”她用冷冷的声音说，“如果你没意见，我想七点出发。”

接着她又出去了。我艰难地从床上爬起来。前一天开了一天车，我浑身酸疼。我快速冲了个冷水澡让自己清醒过来。我穿好了衣服。在我喝咖啡、吃羊角面包时，桑德拉一次次地走进房间，向窗外张望，接着又走出去。

第50页

几分钟后，我从窗户低头往下面的广场看的时候，正巧看到一辆挂着瑞士车牌的银色奔驰在拐角转弯，驶出了我的视野。这样看来安德里亚果然就在附近，我想。又一次。

我想知道我该如何搞清楚怎么回事——直接问桑德拉很难。我环顾房间，检查是否有东西落下，这时我突然看到桑德拉的手机放在椅子上她的外套旁边。

我灵机一动，拿起手机，走进浴室，把它扔进马桶里。这时我听到门开了。我洗了洗手，走回房间。也许那么做是愚蠢的，但我受够了她老是打电话。

“您的司机准备好了，女士。”我对桑德拉说，想开个玩笑。我拿起我们的两个箱子。她笑了——她的笑声听起来很美妙——我们离开了旅馆。

我们开车离开了这个有着暗淡的石头建筑的村庄，路过了我曾和杰基去过的那个美丽的教堂。现在看来那是好长时间以前的事情了。我们在村庄边上停下来加油，不久就回到了E11高速公路，往北驶去。

第51页

我们已经过了克莱蒙–费朗，正逐渐靠近布尔日。什么也没发生。交通正常。我轻松地开着车。天气多云而干燥，没有那两辆车的踪迹。桑德拉也还没注意到她的手机不见了。我们说了些无关紧要的事。我有时向她要她早上买的瓶装水喝。她也隔段时间就给我吃点儿苹果和巧克力。

我边开车边想着到目前为止这次旅行中发生的一切：桑德拉在法国边境时的紧张，那两辆看起来像是在跟踪我们的车，桑德拉好几次走出旅馆房间，她不断在接的电话……

我知道，在我们到英国之前，我得马上弄明白怎么回事。我很高兴桑德拉的手机不在了。那样桑德拉就难以给安德里亚或别人打电话了，也给了我更多找出真相的机会。

突然传来一声尖叫。桑德拉正把东西从她的手提包里掏出来，接着转身去翻后座上外套的口袋，翻看车门储物槽里的地图，又往她的座位下面摸。

第52页

“该死！”她叫道，把手重重地拍在膝盖上的地图上。

“怎么了？”我问，尽力让自己听起来既担忧又无辜。

“我找不着手机了。”她叫道，再次在包里一通乱翻。

“镇定，”我说，“肯定就在身边。别着急，好好找找。”

她又找了一遍，但（当然！）没有用。

“你应该不会知道我的手机在哪儿，是吗？”她转头看着我问道。

“那是你的手机，桑德拉。你总是随身拿着。我没见过。”我回答。

她把东西收回包里，双臂交叉在胸前，一脸铁青地盯着前方没有尽头的高速公路。

第 11 章　得知真相

第53页

一点钟左右我们到了巴黎。桑德拉不想穿过市区，所以我们绕着这个首都城市的东边行驶。我开始在脑海中做着计划。我意识到相比高速公路，在我们现在行驶的普通公路上，我有更多机会弄明白怎么回事。这儿有红绿灯、人群和警察局。总会发生点儿什么对我有帮助的事。如果一片偶然掉落的屋顶瓦片能把我置于如此境地，那么就会有其他意想不到的事情发生，帮我摆脱困境。

我为什么相信会有意想不到的机会来帮助我呢？我不知道。但是确实有。我们越往北走，原本就阴沉的天空越发昏暗，最后下起了雨。开始的时候雨不大，但很快就下大了，我只好马上减速。我把挡风玻璃的雨刷调到双倍速度，而那些开出巴黎的大卡车溅起的水重重地拍打着我的小汽车。

天立刻黑了下来，我们被电闪雷鸣包围着，我只能以不到 20 公里的时速开着车。

第54页

透过雨水，我的车灯照到十字路口的一个标牌，上面有几个小村庄的名字。我知道我们马上要回到主干道上了。我现在必须得做点儿什么了。我认为在乡村小道上，安德里亚和其他人很难跟踪我们，于是我决定冒险试试。

我往后看看是否有车灯。远处有几辆车。我只能看到前方不到五十米的路。当我们靠近十字路口时，我突然转动方向盘，迅速穿过马路，开进了一条乡村小路。此时一辆大卡车刚好从我们后面驶过，响起了刺耳的鸣笛声，闪起了车灯，但我做到了。桑德拉被这突如其来的猛烈转弯甩得东倒西歪。

“你疯了吗?”她坐回原处后叫道，“你差点儿害死我们！赶紧回到刚才那条路上去！”

“不行。”我镇静地轻声说。

“立刻回去！”她大吼，“不然我就……不然我就……”

“不然你就怎样?”我问。她没有回答。外面依然大雨滂沱。我把车又开出了几公里以确保没人跟着我们。然后我把车停在路边。我不知道接下来怎么办。我唯一的想法是桑德拉肯定和安德里亚计划那天晚上见面。

第55页

我觉得桑德拉的“朋友们”现在肯定又担心又怀疑，因为他们没法儿和桑德拉通电话。几乎可以肯定，他们会特别生气。但我突然意识到，如果我的车里有安德里亚和罗韦洛先生想要送到英国的东西，我将是该行动成功的关键。出于某种原因，他们都不能亲自去英国——他们需要别人来做此事。说不定他们已经有了犯罪记录。

“那么，”我们一停下来，桑德拉就说道，“我们现在该怎么办?”

“你想一想吧。”我说着把座椅往后推了推，闭上了眼睛。不一会儿我就听到了桑德拉的哭声。刚开始我不想去理她，但后来再也忍不住了。我转身望着她。

“桑德拉，怎么了？”我边问边碰了碰她的胳膊。她把我推开了。

“别烦我。这一路你除了制造麻烦没干别的。”

第56页

她用手捂着脸，泪流满面，很难理解她在说什么。

“嘿，别这样！”我回答，“一直以来举止奇怪的是你，不是我。”

听到这儿，她哭得更厉害了。

“不是我，”她艰难地说，“是他们逼我这么干的。”

“你是什么意思？”我问，完全被她刚刚说的话弄糊涂了，想听到更多解释。她慢慢克制住哭泣，擤了擤鼻子。她看起来一团糟，眼睛和脸都是红的，脸上的妆成了一条条黑线。她看起来像个迷途的小女孩儿，我突然对她充满歉意。

“你能跟我说说吗？”我非常温和地问，伸手去握住她的手，给她力量。

她开始非常低声地说起来。

“这很难解释，保罗，但你已经知道其中一些事了。我想告诉你里面的事情我一件都不想掺和。都是他。”

“谁？”我问。

“安德里亚。”她回答，又开始哭了起来。等可以说话时，她又继续说起来。

“我父亲是一个成功的商人。他开了一家小公司，是和你在波多菲诺看到的那两个人合伙开的。他们做的是仿古家具的进出口，就是看起来像古董的家具。他们在全球都有生意往来，但重点市场在英国和法国。很长时间以来生意都不错，但大概十年前，事情有些不好做了。”

第57页

“可安德里亚是怎么掺和进来的？”我问，再一次握住她的手。

“生意不景气，我父亲和他的合伙人欠了很多钱，他们觉得可能得关闭公司了。这时他们遇到了安德里亚。他在美国有很好的人脉，那里的仿古家具生意依然很火。看样子安德里亚可以挽救公司，于是我父亲和他的合伙人决定让他试试。”

“他们成功了吗？”我问。

“很成功，”桑德拉回答，“实际上，他们太成功了，所以第一年年底我父亲和他的合伙人让安德里亚也成为了合伙人。大家皆大欢喜——看起来一切都会好起来。安德里亚刚开始时对我们全家都很好，特别是对我。我当时觉得他人很好。”

“他比你大很多，不是吗？”我说。

“是的，保罗，他比我大很多……但是我们谈了一段时间恋爱。我父母对此很高兴。家庭对意大利人而言还是非常重要的。他们觉得安德里亚拯救了他们。他是公司的一部分，他们觉得，在将来的什么时候，他也可能成为这个家的一员。对我而言一切都会很安全。而且我爱他……至少，刚开始我爱过他……”

第58页

她停下来，低下头，脸上露出痛苦的神情。我在她脸上轻轻地吻了一下，然后她继续说道：“但是很快，我父亲开始非常担心公司里发生的事情。从美国进出口的家具比第一年多了，但是赚的钱却比之前多很多。我父亲对此难以理解。新客户所支付的家具钱好像比过去与他合作的那些公司支付的要多得多。

“当然，我们都喜欢增长的利润。我们都得到了想要的车。我父亲买了贝拉维斯塔别墅，忘记了马格雷廖。我母亲得以在房子里摆满她一直想要的玻璃制品和名画。大家都很开心。表面上是这样的，但我父亲在心底知道有什么事不对劲。

“最终，大约两年后，他和另两位合伙人让安德里亚解释一下是怎么回事，这样真相就暴露了。他起初是为公司买卖仿古家具，但后来开始换成了真正的古董椅子和橱柜。这些古董大多是偷来的，但海关官员以为那只是仿制家具。他把大量非常珍贵的意大利古董家具运到了美国。那样做神不知鬼不觉，但显然他只不过是在利用我父亲的公司。他还从美国带回各种各样的艺术品。”

第59页

“我的天啊！”我大叫道，“可你父亲为什么不向警方举报他？”

“他不能，”她非常简单地回答，“你看不出我父亲和他的合伙人也都卷进去了吗？他们是公司的拥有者，他们享受着这些非法买卖带来的利益。连我都小小地参与了其中。我有了好车开、好衣服穿、精彩的假期，还要定期穿过边境去瑞士带东西……”

“什么东西？”我说，我想知道那天我的车里到底有什么。

“哦，通常是古董珠宝——在我叫你开车去卢加诺之前，我在边境被拦下过一次。还好我没带什么。所以安德里亚告诉我要你用车带我过去。海关官员不会怀疑你，而且我们需要快点儿到那儿。那是给一个非常重要的顾客的。”

第60页

“可是如果你们把一切都解释给警察听，他们肯定会理解的。”我开始说。

“哦，保罗，没那么简单，”她大声说，“你难道不明白，尽管我父亲看起来仍然像是公司的老板，但我们都在安德里亚的掌控之中吗？如果有人说了什么，我们所有人都会进监狱的。”

“所以是安德里亚让我开车送你去英国的，是吗？带着……带着……不管车里是什么东西。”我问。

“嗯，我真的很想和你去那儿度假，”她回答，紧张地看着我，“但是两周前美国那边遇到了点儿麻烦，安德里亚说我们必须带些东西走……哦，保罗，我并不想让你卷进来，我真的不想。你一定要相信我！”

“那他们现在为什么还跟踪我们？”我问。

“他们想要确保这次行动成功。当我们发现安德里亚的真面目后，我就和他断绝了关系，所以他并不完全信任我。”

第61页

我这下知道在波多菲诺其中一个保镖凌晨四点在我的车那儿做什么了。我还有一个问题。“我车里是什么？他们在我车里放了什么？”

“我不知道。也许是他们想运出国的油画。”

我看着桑德拉。我能看出她说的是实话，一股暖流涌过我的身体。

“哦，桑德拉！”我轻声说道，用胳膊搂住她，将她拉向我。“我相信你。我还以为一直是你在利用我呢。”

她任我把她搂得紧紧的，我感觉她又哭了。我静静地抱着她，仿佛过了很长一段时间。最终她坐直身子，擦了擦眼睛，看着我。

“没有，保罗。根本没有。从来都没有过！”她说，“我不想让你卷入我们家的任何麻烦事。但是安德里亚说他会告诉警察，我们家所有人都会进监狱，因为所有事情都是以我父亲的名义做的。”说到这里，她的眼泪又出来了，她在我怀中哭个不停。

第 12 章　一个糟糕的早上

第62页

我们坐在我那辆旧车里，停在路边静静地拥抱了很长时间。接着我们开始说话。我们决定最好是返回意大利。我们将回到意大利，找一个安德里亚找不到我们的地方与桑德拉的父亲见面。我们将尽快打电话给罗韦洛先生，解释发生的事情并安排一个见面地点。我们觉得最好是尽量说服他去找意大利警方解释整个情况。我们觉得警方会理解罗韦洛家的问题的。毕竟，做非法买卖的是安德里亚。

雨停了。我们把车停在南面 100 公里处的沙头顿镇的一家小旅馆前时，天色已经暗了。返回的路上花了更多时间，因为我们决定避开高速公路，以防安德里亚和他的朋友在找我们。

冲完澡，换了衣服，我们在楼下餐馆里吃了顿向来味道不错的法式旅馆晚餐。饭间气氛安静。我们都很累，但各自有感到欣慰的地方。桑德拉告诉了我真相，不再需要向我隐瞒发生的事情。而我终于差不多了解了自己被卷入的麻烦事。当然，我们都对接下来的处境感到担忧。我们还要面对许多困难，尤其是如何安全地回到意大利。在小酒吧里喝了两三杯卡尔瓦多斯酒之后，我们早早地睡了。我们整晚都紧紧地相互依偎着，感受着身处同一条船上的新温暖。

第63页

* * *

第二天早上六点半左右，我们被卧室门上响亮的敲击声惊醒。桑德拉艰难地从床上爬起来，走到门口。

“等等，桑德拉……”我喊道，清醒了一点儿，“看看是谁……”

但已为时已晚。就在那一刻，她转动钥匙，门开了。桑德拉被安德里亚从门口径直推到了床上。我在波多菲诺见过的其中一个保镖跟着进来，并把门锁上了。他们俩手里都拿着枪。

第65页

桑德拉朝还在床上的我跟前挪了挪，我用胳膊搂着她。她害怕得浑身发抖，脸色苍白。那两个人站在床尾，瞪着我们，看起来很危险。

“看来，”安德里亚缓慢地说，脸上露出恐怖的笑容，“我们找到咱们逃跑的情侣了。”

他和另外那个人对视后大笑起来。

“可怎么可能……？”我开口说。

“你这愚蠢的英国佬！”那个大块头保镖说，“你觉得我们会让你开着车在欧洲乱跑吗，车里面还载着那么多无价的……”

“说话当心点儿！”安德里亚打断他，“车里有些很值钱的东西，难道我们不得看紧了你们？我们不傻，莫里斯先生！我在波多菲诺时在你的车上装了个很强的无线电信号器，这样我们就总能找到你们了。所以在这里找到你们啦！”安德里亚冷笑着说。

桑德拉转过头看着我，脸上一副“我对此完全不知情”的表情，我握住她的手表示相信她。

“现在穿好衣服，收拾收拾，二十分钟内准备好！”安德里亚命令道，“拔掉电话。”

第66页

大块头保镖把电话线从墙上扯了下来。然后他们都离开了，锁上了卧室的门。我把桑德拉搂得更紧了些，彼此相拥了片刻。

“我们现在怎么办？”她说着站了起来。

“现在我一点儿主意都没有，”我回答，依然惊讶于他们竟然如此轻易地找到了我们，也为没有料到他们会密切监视我们的行踪而生自己的气。正如他们所说，车里不管是什么东西都太珍贵了（保镖用的“无价”一词），不可能不管它。我再一次想知道那东西是什么。我从床上下来，走到行李箱边。

“嗯，我觉得我们最好还是按他们要求的做，”桑德拉说，“我们可以边走边想对策。保罗……”

“嗯？”我转身面对着她，她走到我站的地方。“我真的不知道车里有无线电信号这回事。”她说。

“我知道你不知晓。”我回答，给了她一个微笑，并伸出双手。她握住我的手站着看我。“不管怎样，我有事想告诉你。”

“什么？”她说，脸上露出不确定的神情。

第67页

“桑德拉，我爱你，”我说，接着补充道，“这一切结束后，我想一直和你在一起。我……我……我想娶你。”

不得不说我之前的确没想过结婚的事情，但昨天她和我解释过后，我意识到我真的很爱她。之前我对自己的感觉很不确定，起初是杰基的去世让我迷惘，然后是这个可怕的噩梦。而现在好似一间漆黑的房间里打开了一扇窗，阳光照了进来，我得以看清一切。

“哦，保罗，”她难以置信地看着我说，“我做的这些事给你带来了这么多麻烦，你怎么可能还会爱我呢？况且，我们连如何脱身都不知道。”

“我知道现在看起来不可能，”我回答，把她拉得更近一些，“但我们会没事的。就告诉我一件事：你爱我吗？”

“爱，保罗，我爱你。只是现在看起来这么难……”她不说话了，眼泪涌出了眼眶。我双手捧住她的脸颊，凝视着她的眼睛。

“现在不要哭，亲爱的，”我温柔地说，“我现在需要你的帮助，知道吗？”

第68页

她点点头，笑了。我在她美丽的双唇上亲了亲。

“来吧，”我说，“我们做好准备吧。”

* * *

二十分钟后，我们被保镖赶出了房间，被带到了楼下的停车场。安德里亚在那儿等着我们。他们的车停在我的车两侧。

“现在仔细听着，”安德里亚指着我，用一种不高兴的声音开口说，“你已经给我们制造了足够多的麻烦。这次新的耽搁意味着我们不得不在法国多待一两天。”

“为什么？”桑德拉问。

“因为我们在英国的联系人告诉我们，边境的海关人员会检查进入英国的每个人。显然，他们在寻找某个国际恐怖组织。如果我们今天早上入境就不会有事了，可现在太晚了，都是因为你的男朋友。”

“那我们要怎么办？”我问。

“我们要在法国海边度个小假，莫里斯先生，”安德里亚回答，“我们要开车去迪耶普，在那里等到你可以穿过英吉利海峡去纽黑文。从这里到迪耶普大约有250公里，我们午饭前可以轻松到达那里。我们一起去。亚历桑德拉——你坐我的车，这样你就别再想其他逃跑的鬼点子了。莫里斯先生——你开车跟着我们这位保镖的车走。他的黄色汽车很容易看到，所以你不会搞错的。明白吗？毕竟，你不希望亚历桑德拉出什么事，对吧？”

第69页

“你什么意思？”我问。

“我觉得不需要解释，”安德里亚说着把桑德拉推向他的奔驰车，“只要按照要求的做，一切就不会有事。”

第 13 章　农舍

第70页

我按照他们要求的做了。我向北沿着主干道走在两辆车之间。每次看后视镜，我都能看到桑德拉坐在银色奔驰的前座，在安德里亚身旁。她之前肯定这么做过很多次。

我觉得孤立无援，不知道该做什么，尤其是现在桑德拉没有跟我在一起。这似乎让我失去了思考和行动的能力。而且，无论如何，在安德里亚说了那些话后，我害怕如果我逃跑，他们真的会对她做什么。于是我仿佛在梦中一般浑浑噩噩地开着车。

* * *

我们路过了一个又一个小镇。路很干，交通不是很拥堵，十一点半时我们就驶入了迪耶普的郊区。在那儿，保镖闪灯示意停车并停在了路边；我停在他后面，安德里亚的车过来停在我的正后方。保镖和安德里亚从车里出来，在保镖的车顶摊开地图，商量起来。我转身朝桑德拉笑了笑，她回复了我一个飞吻。

第71页

那两个人决定好怎么走后回到车里，我们又启程了。我跟着那辆黄色的菲亚特跑车进了市中心，然后沿着一条海岸公路一直开到海边附近一所孤零零的旧农舍。保镖转弯驶入车道，然后开进了农舍后面的停车场。我跟着。安德里亚和桑德拉的车开过了房子。我想知道他们去了哪儿，但很快意识到他们是去拿钥匙了。

“好了，你，”他们回来后保镖说，“下车，拿上你的包跟我走。”我照做了。安德里亚带我们从后门进了房子。

“车钥匙。”大块头保镖伸出手命令道。我把钥匙给了他。

“别忘了也拿走他的护照，”安德里亚说，“我已经拿到了亚历桑德拉的。”

“你们两个上楼去。”保镖说。

我们被带到楼上，安置在房屋后部不同的房间里。门被锁上了。

“求你了，”我听到桑德拉喊道，“我要上厕所，而且我又饿又渴。”

“等着。”传来回答的声音。我能听到安德里亚和保镖在楼下说话，但听不清他们在说什么。一段时间后门开了，又重重地关上了，我听到那辆黄色的菲亚特启动了。我从窗户向外望去，看到它开走了。

第72页

大约半小时后车开了回来，很快楼梯上传来脚步声。桑德拉的门被打开了，她被允许去上厕所，之后又被关了起来。接着轮到了我。被再次关起来之前，我得到了两大瓶矿泉水、一些法式面包、一些卡蒙贝尔奶酪和两条巧克力。我坐在床上吃起来。

吃完后我开始认真地检查房间。陈设很简单——一张床、一套桌椅、一个衣柜，屋子中间有一块彩色的地毯。有一扇窗户，可以看到停车场、后面凌乱的花园，以及远处的田野。海在相反的方向。我想着接下来该怎么办。我被监禁起来了，我得逃走。但怎么逃呢？

我走近窗户想打开它，但开不了。我走到门前。门挺厚，而且锁得很紧。我还能做什么呢？墙？我把耳朵贴在我和桑德拉房间之间的墙上，希望能听到点儿什么。什么也听不到。我敲了敲墙，等着。没有回应。我又用力敲了敲，继续等着。这时我听到了回应的敲击声。

第73页

咚、咚，我敲着。咚、咚，她敲着。

"你好。"我说。没有回应，显然墙很厚。没办法从房间里出去。我失望地躺在床上，脑袋枕在双手上，盯着天花板。天花板！天花板中间有一扇门通向屋顶。

我躺着看了一阵天花板上的小门，想着如何上到那儿去。它离地板大约有三米半高。我坐起来环视房间。我把椅子从桌子下抽出来，然后悄无声息地搬起桌子，把它搬到天花板上的门的正下方。我把椅子放在桌边，爬上桌子。天花板就在我头顶了，我举起手臂，推了推那扇刷了漆的木门，但它纹丝不动。我又推了推，这次更用力，门轻微地移动了。我继续用力推。

突然，门被推了上去，发出很大的声音。我站着没动，静静听着，希望楼下的那两个人没有听到。楼梯上没有突然跑动的脚步声，我猜我的运气还不错。接着我把椅子拉到桌子上，小心翼翼地爬了上去。我把木门推到一边，把头和肩膀穿过洞，看着屋顶下面的空间。

第74页

我不知道会有什么，但还是被眼前看到的震惊了。房顶非常高，有两扇窗户，阳光从那儿射进来，照亮了整个中心区域。一头有几个箱子，还有很多旧农具。这栋建筑被当作农舍时，这里可能是一个储物间。可能还有一扇通向外面的门，能把东西从下面拉上来。

我仔细地观察着四周。在我房间的窗户上方，我看到墙上有三道光线，它们呈现出一个双扇门的形状。我正准备上到房顶那儿，突然听到下面有声音。我赶紧把门放回开口处，但无法让它关回到原处！没时间了，因为脚步已经到了楼梯顶部。我从椅子上爬下来，跳下桌子，接着把椅子搬回到地板上。

第75页

我听到有人敲桑德拉的门，保镖用意大利语问她是否需要什么。桑德拉说了些什么，门开了，她被允许再去一趟洗手间。

与此同时，我把桌椅放回它们原来的位置。我躺回床上时，钥匙在门孔里转动起来，大块头保镖走了进来。

我朝他看去，希望他不会抬头看天花板，那上面的门附近有污迹。

“你想要什么吗？”他粗鲁地问。

“是的，我想去洗手间。”

我走到我的箱子那里拿出洗漱包和一条毛巾，出门走到洗手间。我看着镜子里自己的脸。我简直一团糟，早上没有刮胡子，脸上有房顶落下的灰尘，眼睛下面因为睡眠不足和过多的担忧而布满了皱纹。我洗完脸，刮完胡子，感觉好些了。我出来时保镖正坐在走廊的一把椅子上。我经过桑德拉的房间时敲了敲门。

“桑德拉，”我喊道，“你还好吗？”

“保罗，”她的声音传出来，“我还好。你呢？发生什么了？”

第76页

“我还好，”我回答，“我不知道发生什么了。我猜我们只是在等什么时候能过界去英国。我不知道是不是——”

“好了，”保镖说着朝我走来，“够了。回你的房间去。”

我照做了。门又被锁上了，保镖的脚步声消失在楼下。我看了看手表——五点钟。我决定现在先不上屋顶去，我要等到安德里亚和保镖睡觉后再说。我又吃了些面包、奶酪和巧克力。十点钟的时候，保镖又来了一次让我上厕所。我隔着门和桑德拉道了晚安。

第 14 章　逃跑

第77页

回到房间，我翻了翻我的箱子，决定带些什么。我换上了深色的衣服，这样晚上就不容易被发现。接着我把闹钟定在凌晨一点，穿着全套的衣服上了床，关了灯。还好我这么做了。午夜前后，我听到有人上楼的声音。我的门被打开了，灯开了一下，应该是安德里亚或是那个保镖来查看我。

之后我躺在黑暗中等待。我肯定是睡着了，因为一点的闹钟响起时，我突然惊醒了。我在黑暗中坐起来听着动静。静悄悄的。我能听到外面海浪的声音。我从床上下来，重复着下午摆桌椅的动作。接着我把一双运动鞋系在一起，挂在脖子上。只穿袜子声音会小得多，我想。

很快我爬上了屋顶下方的空间。我站起来时，楼板发出了声音。月光穿过窗户照进来，给了我一点光亮。我静静地站了一会儿，好让眼睛适应环境。接着我慢慢地、轻轻地走到那两扇门那儿。下午时我没法儿看到它们如何打开，此时在黑暗里只能全凭触觉。我找到门，用手上下摸索。门中间没有锁和钥匙，于是我的手移动到下面。那儿有个金属的东西。我摸索着转动它，把它向上拉，但拉不动。我用双手用力往上拉，门突然开了，我向后摔倒在楼板上，发出一声响。

第78页

我在那儿躺了有一两分钟，因为刚才的用力快速喘着气。我仔细听着，看刚才的响声有没有惊醒任何人。一片寂静。我站起来推门，门开了，发出可怕的声音——肯定是好几年没打开过了。我又等了等。

房子里依然没有动静。我低头看了看。我估计这儿离地面大概有六七米。我之前没想过怎么下去。我安静地四处走着，看看能不能找到根绳子或梯子什么的来帮我。但什么也没有。我走到门边又低头看了一眼。我想我只能跳了。但我不喜欢跳到坚硬的地面上这个想法。

第79页

我穿上运动鞋，坐在屋顶门边。这儿离地面真的挺高的！我等了片刻，然后跳了下去，在落地的瞬间翻滚了一下。我站起来，拍拍身上的尘土，向我的车走去。车门和后备厢都锁上了。

黑暗中我坐在车旁边，迅速思考该怎么办，并在脑海里列了个清单：第一，回到房子里；第二，找到我的车钥匙，如果可能的话，还有我们的护照；第三，救出桑德拉；第四，逃走。听起来没那么容易！

我深吸一口气，来到房子的后门。令我感到意外的是，门开着。我走进去，依然让门开着，以便必要时快速逃脱。我站在那里听了听，但什么动静也没有。我脱下运动鞋，又挂在脖子上。房子里很黑，我琢磨着是否打开灯找钥匙。

突然楼上传来声响。一扇门开了，我听到走廊上有脚步声。我站着一动不动。洗手间的门开了又关上。我迅速走出门厅来到客厅，透过从窗户射进来的月光，我看到了一张大沙发。我在沙发后面蹲下。我听到冲厕所的声音，接着一盏灯开了，有下楼梯的脚步声。脚步走近时我感觉到背上冷汗都流了下来。客厅的灯开了，有人穿过房间，进了厨房。我听到外面的门关上了。

第80页

我从沙发后张望，审视着房间。一套桌椅、一个壁炉、两把扶手椅、一个显示一点半的大钟、一个壁柜、一台电视机、一个书架……我的眼睛回到了壁柜处，我觉得我在上面看到了几把钥匙和一些证件。

第81页

就在此时厨房传来声音，有人走了出来。我又蹲回沙发后面。灯灭了，脚步声又回到了楼上。我希望他不会去检查我的房间。他没有。

我在沙发后感觉像待了一小时，但实际只有十分钟左右。当感觉可以安全移动时，我悄声来到壁柜处，摸索着找灯亮时看到的钥匙和证件。我拿起它们，走到窗前，在月光下查看。

我吃惊地发现有两套钥匙。一套是我的车钥匙，另一套像是房子的钥匙。更让我惊讶的是，我还发现我们俩的护照也在那儿。我把这些都装到兜里。现在该去找桑德拉了，我想。

出到门厅后我站在黑暗中听着动静。楼上没有任何声音。我开始尽可能慢地走上楼梯，每走一步都停下来等待。我的心剧烈地跳着。最终，我到了楼梯顶端，轻轻地朝桑德拉的房间挪动。我尽量缓慢地在锁眼里转动钥匙，推开门，移身进去，然后关上门。我开了灯。桑德拉在床上坐了起来，双手捂着眼睛。

第82页

“啊，什么人……？”她用意大利语说，声音大得异常危险。我把手指放在我的嘴唇上示意她别出声，她看见了是我。我来到她的床边坐在她身旁。我们拥抱了一会儿。

“可是怎么……？”她又开始说话。

“现在这个不重要，”我低声说，“穿好衣服，把你想要带的尽快装进你的包里。我们这就离开。先别穿鞋。”

她按我说的做了。她准备好之后，我关了灯，我们来到走廊上。我听了一会儿。接着我锁了门，把钥匙从她的门和我的门里拔出来——都是之后能给我们争取时间的事。

我们向楼下缓缓移动，紧张得要命——任何声音都可能会引得那个保镖或安德里亚拿着枪跑出来，那样我们就逃不成了。一下楼来到厨房，我们就都穿上鞋走了出去。我从口袋里掏出房门钥匙，锁上了门，然后把钥匙扔掉了。

第83页

“我们要把车推到马路上，”我一边开车门一边对桑德拉说，“那样我发动引擎时就不会离房子太近了。”

桑德拉同意了。我们把车从两辆车之间推了出来。

“谢天谢地这辆车这么小！”桑德拉隔着车顶低声说。我们轻轻地把车推到了马路上。突然桑德拉转身沿着小路跑了回去，消失了。丢下我一个人在黑暗里。她在干什么？她决定回到安德里亚身边了吗？她要放弃我吗？我突然又开始怀疑起她来。我觉得随时都可能会有灯亮起，有人会朝我开枪。我正准备上车时，看见桑德拉回来了。

“你干什么去了？你去哪儿了……？”我问。

“快，”她说，“上车。”

我们把车又往前推了一点儿，然后跳了进去。车撞到了什么东西，我这侧的车门大声地关上了。我试图发动车子，但没反应。车启动不了。我们面面相觑。我们俩都心惊胆战的。我回头看了看房子，又试着启动车子，还是不行。

一盏灯亮了，朝前的一间卧室的窗户打开了。一个人的脑袋伸了出来，用意大利语喊着什么。我试图再次启动车子。

第84页

“加油啊！”我低声对车子说，第四次尝试。这次车子启动了。这时从房子里传来一声巨响，车后也传来声响。

“快！”桑德拉喊道，“他们在朝我们开枪！”

又是一声枪响，这次在车顶上响了。

“低头趴下。”我说。在我们转过第一个弯前，我一直没开车灯。之后我打开它们，尽力以最快的速度狂奔。我们在路上行驶时还听到了更多的枪声，但没有一发击中车子。

第 15 章　穿越法国南部

第85页

“你回去做什么了？”我朝桑德拉喊道，“你在干什么？我们可能会被抓住的。他们现在很快就会抓住我们了。”我对桑德拉很恼火——不过，如果我想一想，是我的车门关得太响才吵醒了他们。

实际上，桑德拉给我们争取了更多时间。“我割了他们的轮胎。”

她说完举起一把刀。

“你怎么拿到那个的?”我问，感觉开心些了。

“保镖昨晚借给我切面包和奶酪的，”她回答，“我把两辆车的八个轮胎都割破了，所以他们得换轮胎。我猜这能给我们争取到一两个小时的时间，即使他们晚上这会儿能找人出来换轮胎。”

“你真是太棒了，桑德拉·罗韦洛!”我大声喊着。

我此前没想过要去哪里。当我们驶向迪耶普时，我问桑德拉有什么想法。

第86页

“我觉得我们还是要回意大利。”她说。

“好。意大利，我们来了。”

我们往南开，在城外的第一个加油站停下来加油，并买了些吃的和喝的。那是早上五点。我们非常累，但觉得还要继续开。桑德拉睡了一小会儿。大约下午一点，我们又停了下来。我们需要更多的汽油，也需要休息。给车加完油，在酒吧喝了点儿东西后，桑德拉给她父亲打电话说了发生的事。我们约好第二天在意大利边境见面。之后我们把车挪到停车场的角落好去休息一下。

“我们休息一个小时，然后继续赶路。”

我把驾驶座椅往后推了推，我太累了，很快就睡着了。

* * *

我猛地醒了过来。桑德拉睡在我旁边。我看了看手表。“见鬼!”我大叫道，“桑德拉，桑德拉。快醒醒，四点了!”她好不容易才醒过来。

第87页

“怎么了？”她说，“怎么回事？”

“快。我们这就出发。四点了。我们睡得太久了！”我喊道。

我们准备好后立刻出发了。

“我们俩都累坏了，睡得太少，又有太多事情要担心，”开车时我对桑德拉说，“我们会没事的。我确定割坏他们的轮胎给我们争取了需要睡觉的时间。现在我们可以直接开往边境了。”

第 16 章　高速追逐

第88页

但我们忘记了安德里亚在车里放的无线电信号发射器。我们往南开了大约二十分钟，右边是马贡内葡萄酒产区迷人的丘陵，这时我突然在后视镜里看到远处有个黄色的东西。随着它越来越靠近，我认出那是辆黄色的菲亚特跑车。我的心里一阵难受。

“桑德拉，”我轻声说，“看我们后面。”

她转过身。“哦，不！”她说，“可他是怎么发现我们的呢？”

“嗯，别忘了他的车开起来有我的两倍快，”我回答，“而且他还能用无线电信号跟踪我们。”

“安德里亚也在！”她突然喊道，“看！在那辆比利时卡车后面。”

我看了看后视镜。那辆银色奔驰正在超越一辆大卡车。我的心跳差点儿停止。我们现在怎么办？这时我有了个主意。

第89页

“给我看下地图，桑德拉。”我赶紧说。她展开地图，把手指放在第戎上，这样我就能更容易地看到我们现在的位置。

“好。我们别按原计划离开高速公路了。我们继续向南，沿着A6公路往里昂方向开。”

“可我们为什么要那样做？”她疑惑地问，“他们的车都比我们的快得多。”

“这就是问题的关键，”我解释说，“如果我们离开高速公路，就会是山路，而这辆小车爬山不太行，那样他们要抓住我们就轻而易举了。而且，那条路上车辆不多，没多少警察和其他人可以帮我们。我要做的就是在这条平坦的高速公路上尽可能快速开。他们只能跟着。希望警察能很快注意到这些车都开得太快了。一旦看到警察跟着，我们就停下来，你用你美妙的法语解释来龙去脉。这是目前我们唯一的机会了，桑德拉。不然安德里亚就会阻止我们，为所欲为。”

“可是，保罗，那很危险。”她说，眼睛里露出担心的神情。

“可这并不比被安德里亚和那个大块头保镖抓住更危险，对吧？”我问。

第90页

“对，我想是的，”她回答，“但是小心点儿，保罗。”

我亲了亲她的脸。在后视镜中，我能看到保镖开的黄色菲亚特在后面和我隔着两辆车，安德里亚的奔驰又隔了大约四辆车。我在中间车道，路上车不多。

“好，”我说，“我们出发吧。”

我开得越来越快。我从未真正想过要试试我的宝驰车到底能跑多快——记速器显示是每小时180公里，但我之前从没开过时速超过130公里。很快我就在高速公路的快车道上以每小时170公里的速度行驶。我打开了车灯，让警示灯也闪起来。

“我觉得你最好别再快了。”桑德拉在汽车引擎的轰鸣中紧张地叫道。显然我的车子不喜欢这样。

“没事，”我大声回答，“这样没关系。他们跟着呢。”

两辆车都超过其他车跟在我们后面，相距几百米，这会儿安德里亚的奔驰刚好跑到黄色菲亚特前面了。

“看！”桑德拉兴奋地指着上方喊道，“前面桥上有辆警车。”我们往桥上开时我闪了好几次车灯，希望引起他们的注意。

第91页

此时安德里亚紧紧地跟着我，也闪着车灯。桑德拉望过去时，他挥挥手臂，指向路边。

“他在示意我们靠边停车，”她说，“他肯定是疯了！”

第92页

“你能看到那个保镖吗？”我问。我在后视镜里只能看到安德里亚。

“能，他在安德里亚后面大约一百米。而且……”她深吸了一口气，“保罗，保罗……后面也有一辆警车，我能看见蓝色的警灯。你的计划成功了！”

我试图让我的宝驰车跑得再快些。我的前方没有什么车，其他前面的车在我闪灯的时候都移到中间车道了。我们现在的时速超过180公里了，引擎发出可怕的声音，整辆车都在抖动。在下一个路口，桑德拉看见又有两辆警车加入了这场追逐。

她看了看安德里亚，他就在后面不到二十米远处跟着我们，她用意大利语咒骂了他。他又发出了信号。中间车道有了空间，我没有减速就换了车道。安德里亚紧跟着。

接着我开入应急车道，依然那么快。路面不是很好，轮胎发出很大的噪声。

“小心，保罗，”桑德拉转回身来面向前方时惊恐地大声喊道，“看前面！”

第93页

在远处，我看见一辆大卡车停在应急车道上。它在快速向我们靠近。

“哦老天！”我喊道，开始减速。后面立刻发出碰撞的巨响，我的车被猛烈地往前撞了一下。桑德拉尖叫起来，尽管有安全带，我们俩都往前摔去。在我突然减速时安德里亚撞到了我们的后面。他没有看到前面怎么回事。我迅速用力踩住刹车，升起一团橡胶燃烧的烟气和尘土，但是为时已晚。

我和宝驰车没能避开撞上了那辆卡车。车停住时向右拐了，整个车的左边——桑德拉那边——猛烈地撞上了卡车尾部，发出一声可怕的金属撞击声，桑德拉长长地尖叫了一声。然后一切都安静下来。

* * *

我醒来时躺在一辆救护车里。我试着坐起来，但没成功。旁边有位护士。我问她的第一件事是：“桑德拉在哪儿？”那位表情严肃的法国护士点了点头。我又昏迷了过去。

第 17 章　现在的生活

第94页

现在我坐在这里，望着外面美丽的湖面。夏日的太阳正在落下，在水面上映出长长的橙色倒影。我想说，在某种程度上，那天我生命中的太阳也落下去了。我能讲的还有很多，但我想我应该告诉你们故事的结尾。

我的车撞到了卡车尾部，我只受了几处轻伤，但桑德拉的伤势要严重一些。她在医院住了几个月，我大部分时间都守在她的床边。

安德里亚撞上我的车尾后，他那辆奔驰失去了控制，冲出高速公路的边缘，然后撞上了一棵树。他当场死亡。后来警方认出他是安德里亚·达卡尔塔，也叫安德鲁·卡德，还叫卡特·安德鲁斯。国际刑警组织知道他，还因为好几起在欧洲和美国发生的影响较大的艺术品盗窃案而通缉他。

那个保镖因为开黄色的菲亚特跑车开得太快而被法国警察拦下。他们发现他为安德里亚工作，帮安德里亚盗窃艺术品。最后他被判入狱十年。之后马格雷廖的房子被搜查，发现了许多被盗的画作、雕塑和古董珠宝。

第95页

当我的车被仔细搜查时，他们发现了三幅国际知名的油画，是从意大利和美国偷来的。

我和桑德拉都被允许自由离开了，不过法国警察告诉我以后开车时要更加小心。之后，在意大利，安德里亚和他的生意信息曝光后，警方认同罗韦洛先生和他的合伙人之前是处于非常艰难的处境。大多数被盗的家具和画作都被找到了，罗韦洛先生又重新做起了他的仿古家具生意。

你们可能已经猜到了，桑德拉身体好些后我们就结婚了。不幸的是，我们的婚姻没有持续很久。也许我们只是不同类型的人，也许是因为她和她的家人所陷入的处境，也许是因为法国那场可怕的车祸……不论是什么原因，那场车祸后我们之间有了隔阂，而且这种隔阂似乎与日俱增。

于是在我们结婚一年后，我们同意分居几个月，看看是否有帮助。但那没什么效果，于是我们决定离婚。我们离婚大约一年后，桑德拉嫁给了个医生，他们移居到了美国。

第96页

我再次决定留在科莫。就像杰基去世时一样，我觉得自己想留在意大利。意大利是杰基喜欢过的地方之一，也是我依然热爱的地方。也可能是因为意大利让我想起了杰基，我才留在了这里。于是我买下了科莫湖边这座可爱的老房子。杰基会喜欢这儿的……

现在我回想起来，我和杰基之间的爱是美好的、纯真的……即使这么多年后，我仍怀念那份爱，那份纯真的爱……

和桑德拉的历险之后，我继续在科尔沃制药公司工作。但离婚后不久，我就创办了自己的公司。我在家里通过电子邮件、网络、电话和传真来经营它。

这些日子我基本都是一个人过。在许多方面我的生活相当轻松。我有大量的时间去思考事情是如何运作的。我思考过人类与我们居住的这个地球之间的关系，我也试图理解一切皆因机缘巧合……

一片屋顶的瓦片掉了。

一片屋顶的瓦片待在原处。